Wicked
DENVER

Wicked DENVER

Mile-High Misdeeds and Malfeasance

Sheila O'Hare and
Alphild Dick

THE
History
PRESS

Published by The History Press
Charleston, SC 29403
www.historypress.net

Copyright © 2012 by Sheila O'Hare and Alphild Dick
All rights reserved

First published 2012

Manufactured in the United States

ISBN 978.1.60949.153.6

Library of Congress CIP data applied for.

Contents

Introduction

Denver, without doubt, is the wickedest place, according to its population, on the globe.
—Silverton Standard, *March 5, 1904*

First, an explanation of what this book is and what it is not. *Wicked Denver* is in no way a comprehensive guide to crime in the city and county. Rather, it is an attempt to focus on some of the lesser-known but representative offenses of the time period selected (roughly, 1870 to 1930). It is unapologetically a partial and idiosyncratic selection; our approach is episodic rather than comprehensive and continuous. Nonetheless, we believe that the cases and themes discussed in the book are worthy of further examination and contextualization; within the constraints of our format, we believe that readers will find the material interesting and sometimes surprising. Some cases have drawn little attention from previous historical researchers, possibly because they involved sexual offenses, prominent families or unique circumstances; a few are better-known but too relevant to omit.

"Denver," first a part of Arapahoe County and then, in 1902, established by referendum as the city and county of Denver, has been interpreted flexibly here to include the metropolitan area; thus readers will find references to a few cases that arose in the adjacent Adams (also formerly part of Arapahoe County) and Jefferson Counties. The chapters are based on persistent themes in news reportage over the period: poisonings, domestic killings, juvenile offenses, street and saloon life, money disputes, murder-suicides, insanity and unsolved murders, as well as a glance at some routine lesser offenses (larceny, forgery and so on).

Most of the cases discussed here involve homicides. A very brief discussion of sentencing laws in the period may be helpful. Colorado's mandatory capital punishment law for first-degree murder was enacted in 1883, repealed in 1897 and restored in 1901. The repeal, some scholars have argued, was driven by the state's desire to shed its lawless frontier image; the 1901 reinstatement was based on the theory that the state-sanctioned penalty would prevent vigilantism and lynchings (the particularly gruesome lynching of John Porter in Limon in 1900 was influential in the decision). After 1901, first-degree murder could be punished by death or life imprisonment. Defendants in homicide cases over the period tended to be charged with the generic "murder," though first-degree (premeditated) murder, second-degree murder and voluntary or involuntary manslaughter were the statutory choices. Voluntary manslaughter encompassed killings in the "heat of passion," arising from provocation; involuntary manslaughter encompassed unintentional homicides. Penalties for manslaughter were, not surprisingly, much lighter, ranging from less than a year to eight years.

Due to space limitations, detailed citations have been omitted. Denver newspapers (the *Rocky Mountain News*, the *Post*, the *Republican* and so on) are generally referred to without repetition of the location prefixes; non-Denver newspaper names are given in full.

Chapter 1
Saloons and Street Life

Saloons were community hubs in frontier cities, and Denver was no exception. Thomas J. Noel's *The City and the Saloon* (1996) is the definitive source on the saloon culture of Denver. In the city's early life, saloons served multiple purposes as gathering places—hotels, business centers, restaurants, theaters and even mortuaries. As Noel noted, Denver's gender imbalance until 1870 (men outnumbered women six to one) contributed to the growth and vigor of the city's street life. Holladay Street (later renamed Market) was the city's red-light district. Some of the saloons, blackguards, madams and "girls" of Market Street are well known; here are some less familiar cases that are equally revealing of this side of Denver life.

HARRY TRAVILLA

"A house of ill-fame is veritably an alluring gateway to hell."

The August 18, 1880 murder of Abram M. Marburger (aka Solomon), age unknown, a traveling salesman for Abel Brothers Tobacco Company, in Carrie Smith's "bagnio" (brothel) is a fairly typical example of an alcohol-fueled brawl. Harry Travilla (aka Henry R. Travilla, Travelli, Newman or Harry Hill), a twenty-three-year-old clerk, was Smith's lover. He had come to Denver in February from Leavenworth, Kansas. The *St. Louis Globe-Democrat* noted that he had been known there as "a regular sport, driving fast horses, associating with bloods and fast women generally, and spending a good deal of money."

The incident occurred during a quarrel at Smith's establishment at 487 Holladay Street, and it received national attention. The *Rocky Mountain News* noted that "it was almost impossible to get anything like a connected statement from the inmates of the house…it was very evident that the whole party knew a great deal more than they would tell." This reference included Smith and the girl who had been in a room earlier with Marburger, one Kitty Campbell. Reporters eventually extracted the story of one of the most ridiculous arguments to ever end in murder. Marburger was fanning himself with a small advertising fan; Campbell asked him to give it to her, and he refused. She grabbed the fan and ran off with it. He pursued her and took it back but was angry and erupted into a tirade. Smith interceded and struck Marburger with an empty beer bottle pulled from a basket near the door. Marburger "struck her slightly, and she fell over against the casing of the door." Then a partially dressed man rushed down the stairs, carrying a .44-caliber revolver. He shot Marburger in the head, and the victim died at the scene.

The shooter was Travilla, and he ran through the back door and disappeared (not, the papers noted, taking the time to dress or put on his boots). The women were held as accessories. Smith was "a small woman of blonde proclivities, and, while seemingly very quiet in her demeanor, has the reputation of being a degenerate woman who has threatened to shoot more than one man." Campbell, "a brunette with a very dissipated face," was also reported to have struck Marburger with empty bottles.

An editorial in the *News* bemoaned the presence of such "bagnios" in Denver, stating:

> It is fearfully rough on any man to get killed in a den of prostitution, for it advertises the fact that he has been to such places…A house of ill-fame is veritably an alluring gateway to hell. It is the shame and disgrace of our commercial life that they are chiefly sustained by the patronage of commercial drummers [traveling salesmen] and their country customers. Drummers who are virtuous and reliable men often find themselves compelled to show their customers the town, and to be able to do so must be on familiar terms with the leading courtesans. It was this necessity of his occupation that furnishes the only extenuation we can think of for poor Marburger.

Travilla, who had left town, was apprehended on September 16, 1881, in Milwaukee and returned to Denver for trial, which took place in October. He claimed that he was awakened by the fight, grabbed the gun and

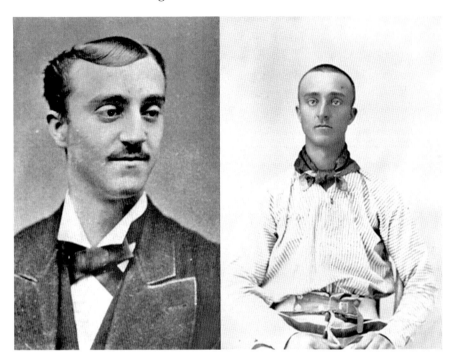

Harry Travilla, before and after conviction. *Sam Howe Collection, Colorado Historical Society; Colorado State Archives.*

confronted Marburger, demanding, "What's all this fuss about?" Marburger struck him "over the eyes." Travilla then hit Marburger on the head with the muzzle end of the revolver. "When it went off I was horror struck," Travilla said. He ran outside and hid in a stable, returning later for his things and money that Smith owed him, and then left town. He pleaded not guilty. The jury received a set of instructions that almost compelled the members to exonerate Travilla and the women; after coming back with a "faulty" verdict, they were sent back to deliberate again and found Travilla guilty of manslaughter. The case against the women was dismissed.

Travilla was sentenced to five years in the penitentiary at Canon City. His conduct was "most exemplary," and Warden C.P. Hoyt supported his application for a pardon. The argument now was that he had been an industrious man of good reputation until he fell in with bad companions; his widowed mother needed his support, and he was promised a job in his hometown of Leavenworth upon his release. (This view of Travilla's character, of course, contradicted all earlier reports.) Governor James B. Grant pardoned Travilla on June 11, 1884.

THE FITZGERALD CASE

"A mighty funny time to clean carpets."

One of the better-known saloon cases was the murder of John H. Fitzgerald, a "colored" barber from Leadville, by Belle Warden, age twenty-five, proprietress of a Denver brothel; Mattie Lemens (aka Lemmon or Lemmens), prostitute, age thirty-two; Berry Gates (aka Barry Gage or W.B. Gates), Lemens's lover; and Charles Smith (real name Anthony Delp, nicknames "Dutch" and "Cottonhead"), age twenty-eight, hack driver and Warden's lover.

On March 18, 1884, Fitzgerald's body was found in the bed of Cherry Creek. At the outset of the investigation, the cause of death was unclear. Fitzgerald, a "nicely dressed, good looking" man, was last seen leaving George Lyons's gambling saloon at 385 Holladay Street, where he lost twenty dollars in a game of faro. He was thought to have had a bankroll of several hundred dollars on his person.

Suspicion soon fell on Warden, Lemens, Gates and Smith. Gates had already served time in prison for burglary and was suspected in the 1882 murder of butcher Jacob Daub, though he had never been charged in that case. Warden had been charged with keeping a disorderly house, Lemens was a known prostitute and Smith was closely associated with the other parties. Detectives believed that the four had followed Fitzgerald and convinced him to visit Warden's house at 578 Holladay Street (described by the *Rocky Mountain News* as a "coon dive"). Then, "the services of a woman there, the paramour of Gates [Lemens], were enlisted to detain Fitzgerald and drug him. Beer was drunk by the park, and Fitzgerald, who had been drinking somewhat, was either made dead-drunk or drugged, probably the latter." It was suspected that he was murdered in his sleep by the group for his money and possessions early in the morning, his body being moved by Gates and Smith to a shed in Warden's yard before being deposited in Cherry Creek.

Fitzgerald's autopsy revealed several contusions on the head and a stab wound to the chest, which the physician opined was produced by a double-edged knife. At the coroner's inquest in June 1884, each of the parties seemed eager to place the blame on the others. Gates denied any knowledge of the murder but testified that Warden had told him that detectives were looking for him and that he should leave town "so she could shoulder the murder on him." Lemens "appeared to be afflicted with a very bad memory at first" but then described Warden as fainting; then she cried and wrung her hands after learning that Fitzgerald's body had been found. "She said she was ruined for life, and

Charley Smith (left) and Berry Gates (right). *Colorado State Archives; Sam Howe Collection, Colorado Historical Society.*

Mattie Lemens, before and after conviction. *Sam Howe Collection, Colorado Historical Society; Colorado State Archives.*

Belle Warden, before and after conviction. *Sam Howe Collection, Colorado Historical Society; Colorado State Archives.*

said she wouldn't have cared if it hadn't been done at her house." Smith stated that "there wasn't enough money in Colorado to induce him killing a man" and that Warden's behavior was not unusual—she often had fainting fits. Mabel Rivers, a former inmate of Warden's house, testified that Warden was afraid of Gates, "as she did not like to have him around and slept with her trunk against the door," and said that Gates had told her that he "had once killed a man and had him buried up in Cherry Creek, and would do it again."

Other physical evidence was incriminating. A gunnysack was found near the Platte River containing a bloody comforter and a bloody bearskin; a chambermaid identified the comforter as Lemens's and the sack as Warden's. The bearskin, she thought, might have belonged to Smith; Gates, not surprisingly, readily confirmed the identification.

Additional testimony was given by the victim's wife; George Lyons, owner of the gambling saloon, as well as his employee, G.W. Woods; and Isaac Gilmore, an owner of another saloon. They confirmed Fitzgerald's whereabouts and the events of the evening before his departure. The madam of a nearby house, Lizzie Archer, corroborated the prosecution's argument that Fitzgerald was murdered early in the morning, testifying that "about 1 or 2 o'clock in the morning, in the middle of March last, she heard cries of murder, emanating from Belle Warden's place, and about fifteen minutes later, she heard someone walk past her house." She also stated that when she visited Warden's place the next day, "Warden took up carpets, and I thought it was a mighty funny time to clean carpets."

At trial in early November, the jury found Warden, Lemens, Gates and Smith guilty of second-degree murder. Each of the four suspects was sentenced to ten years in prison for his or her involvement in Fitzgerald's death, regarded as a comparatively light sentence. There was some dispute over the fact that the verdict was not murder in the first degree, but according to the judge, "There was nothing in the evidence that whether there had been malice or malicious intent in the killing." Warden, the *News* reported, had "another crying spell": "There have been rumors that Belle Warden, who is inclined to be very hysterical, had made a partial confession…but there was nothing in her actions yesterday to indicate this." The defendants all professed their innocence once more before the sentence was pronounced.

In April 1886, the *News* reported that Smith was working in the limekiln at the prison and "appears satisfied with his work." Lemens was doing laundry work. Warden "is behaving well but thinks Warden [R.A.] Cameron a little too much of a preacher to suit her ideas." Lemens died in prison on May 8, 1887. Smith, who was occasionally referred to as a dupe of the other parties, was pardoned on April 28, 1890.

We have another small view of Warden in the penitentiary. In February 1889, she approached a reporter from the *News* who was touring the prison and asked him to correct a statement published about Lemens's death. "She stated that Mattie made no confession and that she fell dead when getting up from the table after eating her dinner. Belle's anxiety to have a denial made may be explained by the fact that she is endeavoring to secure a pardon." Warden was discharged (not pardoned) on March 18, 1891. Gates, after a reduction in his sentence of three years for good behavior, was released in 1891 and resurfaced in Salt Lake City, Utah. In June 1894, he reappeared in the court on charges related to a brawl with Mrs. Sarah Shepard, probably a prostitute. Incidentally, in May of the same year, he won third prize in a cakewalk contest.

ANNIE TRESIZE

"I am done with all this business—I guess my race is run all right."

Annie Tresize (née Miller, aka Laura Trezeis, Trezies, Flo Summers or Frazier), age twenty-nine, was arrested on Market Street and fined fifty dollars and costs for vagrancy on August 21, 1896. The *Denver Post* took the opportunity to relate some details of her past, noting that she was "well known to the police of this and all the principal cities in Colorado." Describing her as "a shining light among the demi-monde" twenty years earlier, she had lived in Leadville, Pueblo and Colorado Springs.

In 1893, she was in Gunnison, where she married a man named Tresize. He left her within a short time, and she went back to a life of prostitution. Tresize became acquainted with two men, Fred Brimer (aka Bremer) and Fred Jackson; in early 1894, both called on her, and a drunken fight took place. Brimer knocked Tresize down on a hot stove and beat her badly. She pulled a revolver from a bureau drawer and fired it at Brimer; the bullet went through the fleshy part of Brimer's arm and then into bystander Jackson's chest, instantly killing the latter. Tresize was found guilty of involuntary manslaughter and, on May 22, was sentenced to two years in the state penitentiary. She was discharged on April 8, 1896.

Upon her release, Tresize went to Colorado Springs, where she met up with John Woods, age thirty-one, the "colored desperado," a man she had met in prison. Woods was famous for a homicide at the Parlor Grove at Thirty-second and Larimer Streets on July 24, 1885. The occasion was a ball given by prostitute Lizzie Archer (also mentioned in the Joos case, discussed

Annie Tresize. *Colorado State Archives.*

later). Woods escorted Melinda Scott; she flirted with Fred Sanders and aroused Woods's jealousy. Woods shot Sanders, who died at his home the next day. Woods admitted to the shooting but claimed that he had acted in self-defense. At trial, he was found guilty of voluntary manslaughter and sentenced to eight years in prison. At the time of the offense, the *News* noted that "Woods had been a hard working man and bore a much better reputation before the homicide than the man who was killed. Sanders was rather of the vagrant and tin-horn order of humanity."

Woods's reputation took a nosedive thereafter. When released from prison, he became involved in a brawl at Smith's saloon on the corner of Market and Twentieth Streets. The date was July 4, 1891, and he was drinking with William Wallace. The two argued about who should settle the bill with the bartender. Woods stabbed Wallace, but the latter recovered; the former was sent to county jail for four months. In February 1895, Woods returned to the penitentiary for burglary for a year; he had broken into the Colorado Carriage Company and left his pipe behind. He met Tresize in the penitentiary. Once released, the couple seems to have spent as much time in jail as they did in each other's company.

Tresize came to Denver about a month before the vagrancy offense, at Woods's insistence, but about ten days later he was back in the county jail for harness thefts. She remained in Denver, but her problems continued. She attacked her landlord on Market Street with a knife and was sentenced to a year in prison, but the sentence was suspended, apparently owing to her poor health and hospitalization. Then she was arrested at Nineteenth and Market Streets for larceny from the person. In court on July 30, 1897, she was "utterly indifferent and careless" and "bowed and threw a rather angry kiss" in the direction of the judge. He queried her, "You have been rather a bad woman?" Annie replied, "Well, I ain't been any angel, your honor." "We will put you out of the way where you won't annoy people anymore," the judge responded, sentencing her to three years in prison.

Interviewed in jail by the *Denver Post*, she was in tears. "I am done with all this business—I guess my race is run all right," she said, musing on her high times in California and Aspen, "until all my friends went back on me." She expressed great regret over the shooting of Jackson and recalled how she had to be smuggled out of Gunnison, as "the miners wanted to lynch me."

Woods, out of jail only two weeks, was arrested again on September 5, 1897, while burglarizing Michael Keefe's store at 2753 Larimer. He stole two pairs of shoes.

IDA JONES

"I never had a father or mother to teach me the difference between right and wrong."

Ida Jones was one of the best-known women of Market Street. Nicknamed "Black Ide," she made frequent appearances in the Denver newspapers. In March 1889, she was arrested for making a violent scene at a dressmaker's shop on the corner of Nineteenth and Larimer Streets when a dress she had ordered turned out to be (in her words) "a beastly fit." In the fall of the same year, she became involved in an exchange of threats with Blanche Hoskell and returned to court, and then she was arrested for maintaining a house of prostitution. Jones was described consistently as "of a quarrelsome disposition"; opinions of her appearance ranged from "rather prepossessing looking" to "tall and coarse looking." Thanks to her criminal career, several photographs of Ida have survived.

In March 1890, she was tried on malicious mischief charges for throwing bricks and stove lids through the windows of the residence of Lizzie (aka Alsie) Ames, "a German negress, having been born on the Rhine…to add to her strange existence, she married a white man from Missouri." According to one report, both women were fined ten dollars, since Ames had responded in kind. Released from jail on bond, she immediately became involved in an affray at the United States Hotel on Blake near Twentieth Street and was rearrested. In April, she struck William Muse on the head with a potato masher; both parties were arrested.

On August 1, 1890, Ida stabbed and killed Stephen Zimmer, a stonemason, at Twentieth and Market Streets. Zimmer was described as being "fond of his beer." Jones claimed that Zimmer had struck her and cut her dress with a knife and then tried to hit her with a rock before she stabbed him. One

Ida Jones, chronologically from left to right. *Colorado State Archives.*

witness to the incident, a shoeshine boy named Willie Johnson, reportedly said that Zimmer had something in his hand when the attack occurred, but no weapon was found by police at the site. (One wonders if a rock would have drawn their attention in any case.)

The accuracy of the report may be questionable; at the inquest, the only witness to the stabbing who testified was newsboy James Brown, age ten, who said that Jones had "run up" to Zimmer and stabbed him as he walked down the street. Moreover, "the dead man did not do anything and he did not have anything in his hands when she struck him." The *Rocky Mountain News* also mentioned that "the colored women who live in the houses of ill fame on the row say they are frequently imposed on and abused by white men who frequent such places so that some of the girls had armed themselves for just such men." In any event, Jones's self-defense claim was given little credence.

Zimmer was brought to the city hospital, where he was pronounced dead; his pockets contained recent letters from his wife in Hastings, Nebraska.

Ida pleaded not guilty, but her reputation for violent aggression made an acquittal unlikely. Moreover, as historian Anne M. Butler noted, the appearance of two members of the prominent white Wallace-Ryan family probably stacked the deck against her. While the authorities turned a blind eye to much of the city's vice and disorder—especially when it remained confined to the fringe community—Jones had become a problem beyond the Market Street milieu.

She was found guilty of second-degree murder. Ida expressed remorse at her sentencing, stating, "I did not mean to kill him. I am sorry, but I cannot bring back the life I took." On October 31, 1890, she was sentenced to fifteen years in prison. We have an incidental glimpse of Jones's early days at the state penitentiary; a woman reportedly named Anna Frazier (or Frieze), having been sentenced to a repeat stint there in July 1897, told the *Post* that "I [*sic*] just as soon go back to the pen as not if it wasn't for that big nigger woman, Ida Jones, who is serving a life sentence [*sic*] for killing a white man in Denver. She and I were always fighting and Warden Cleghorn just lets her have her own way." Anna Frazier was actually Annie Tresize; clearly, both remained too strong-willed for their own good.

Jones applied for pardon in 1895, arguing that her improved conduct in prison and her troubled life ("I never had a father or mother to teach me the difference between right and wrong") warranted an early release. She was not discharged until August 1899, having served eight years. Jones retained her combative character after her release. She returned to her old haunts, taking up residence at Market Street once more, and was soon arrested for striking Jennie Thompson, another denizen of the street, with a baseball bat at the corner of Twenty-first and Market. After she robbed a Swedish man, Charles Peterson, of $200, she was sentenced on March 22, 1902, to five to ten years in prison for larceny from person. She was then thirty-five years old and pregnant. Discharged on July 9, 1908, her trail ends.

THE DEATH OF WILLIAM JOOS

"They did not understand the deadly effect of morphine and gave him too much."

Ardell Smith (aka the "Yellow Kid"), age seventeen, was a "remarkably beautiful octoroon," according to the *Rocky Mountain News*. The paper zealously followed her exploits, and 1891 was an active year for Ardell. Along with one Gertie Green, she appeared in the *News* on January 30, 1891, charged with vagrancy. On February 26, 1891, she returned to the spotlight again, this time with a five-inch gash on her left arm; she and Ida Dayton, who ran a brothel at 2242 Market Street, had a street fight over a Pullman porter named Gus Lewis during which "the Dayton girl produced a knife and began carving her adversary." Ardell was stitched up by the police surgeon and sent on her way.

In May 1891, Ardell found herself in trouble again. On the twenty-seventh, Golden Brewery employee William Joos (aka Joss or Noste), age unknown, died after drinking beer in a "dive" at 2235 Market Street. The madam of the house, Blanche Morgan (aka Pearl Smith or Cora Smith), age twenty-two; a girl named Mattie Fisher, age twenty; and Ardell were charged with murder.

The facts of the case were hardly unusual and were actually reminiscent of the Fitzgerald case. Joos, carrying about fifty-five dollars on his person, arrived at 2235 Market at about 3:00 p.m. and accompanied Ardell to her room. A short time later, Ardell called to Blanche and gave her a quarter to buy some beer. Blanche sent a porter, Lonnie Hannibal, on the errand and then returned to chatting with three friends—Fannie Nash, Annie Mitchell and Mollie White—visiting from other Market Street abodes. Blanche complained of a headache and asked Mollie White if she had some morphine with her. Mollie, one of Ida Dayton's girls and a "morphine fiend," handed Blanche the box containing her supply. Blanche took a large pinch, which she held in her hand until the beer arrived. She drank with the other women and then went back to the room occupied by Joos and Ardell. She was gone long enough that the visiting women departed, as did Mattie Fisher, a resident of the house.

"What happened after Blanche went into the room," the *News* reported, "is not known, but it is naturally supposed that they dosed the beer given to Joss [Joos] and administered it to put him to sleep for the purpose of robbing him. They did not understand the deadly effect of morphine and gave him too much." The women allegedly removed Joos's cash and ejected the drowsy man into the street.

William Joos.

Joos wandered into a 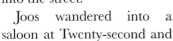 saloon at Twenty-second and Market, where he vomited and fell into a stupor. Police were called, and Joos was removed to headquarters, where he was treated by the police surgeon. Joos initially appeared to rally but then relapsed and died at 8:40 p.m. in the county hospital. He was, however, able to make a statement in which he said that women in "a colored house" had poisoned him. He claimed to have been robbed of fifty-five dollars.

Blanche, Ardell and Mattie Fisher were promptly arrested. Blanche and Ardell staunchly denied knowing the deceased and denied seeing him at their house; Mattie, however, described what she had seen before she left the house and identified Joos as their visitor. Blanche reportedly interrupted Mattie with the words, "You black [expletive deleted in original], this may cost me ten years, but don't fear, I'll meet you at the end of that time."

Police were able to obtain corroboration from Mitchell, Nash and Mollie White, along with the box containing the morphine. More details concerning the principal actors in the case became available as well. Joos had been married for two years and had a young child, but he and his wife had "never lived together happily." When Mrs. Joos heard the details of how and where her husband died, she refused to let the body be brought home and declared that "she does not care how or by whom he is buried." News reports identified Blanche Morgan as the sister of Emma Ford, "the most notorious colored woman in Chicago"; the latter was often found in the Illinois courts for her involvement in brawls and assaults.

The case went to trial in September. Blanche retained Denver's most famous defense attorney, Edgar Caypless, who asked for and received a separate trial for his client. Blanche, easily the most intelligent of the women, had also managed to shift a portion of the blame to other parties. Despite Mattie Fisher's cooperation with the authorities, she found *herself* on trial with Ardell on one count of murder and one count of robbery. By Blanche's account, Joos came in with Mattie, "and she took him into the bedroom to go to bed with him and in a few minutes Mattie came out & sent Ardell Smith in to him"; this may have implied a conspiracy between the two women.

Less effectively, Ardell's lawyer, Willis Stidger, referred to his client's "fatal gift of beauty" and urged the jury to avoid being prejudiced for or against her on that account. Both women were convicted on September 29 of involuntary manslaughter and sentenced to one year of imprisonment in the county jail. The judge noted that all three women appeared to be equally guilty (though Blanche was not yet on trial), and he also commented that "Mattie Fisher has a husband, and if I were sure he would take her back it would have some effect on my sentence. I think, though, she will be a better wife to him after she has passed a year in jail."

For reasons unknown, the case against Blanche was dismissed. She was subsequently convicted of robbery in Chicago and sentenced to five years

Ardell Smith (left), Mattie Fisher (center) and Blanche Morgan (right). *Sam Howe Collection, Colorado Historical Society.*

in the state penitentiary in Joliet, Illinois. She was thought to have aided her well-known and frequently arrested sister in the commission of several similar crimes.

ROBERT HYNDMAN

"I'll never take another thing over a bar."

On March 20, 1902, twenty-four-year old James E. Quinn was killed as a result of a dispute with Robert Hyndman, age twenty-seven, a wagon driver for Bussey Bakery. Quinn, employed by the Denver Gas and Electric Company as a meter inspector, was regarded by friends, family and colleagues as a reputable young man. He lived with his parents at 1142 South Tenth Street; on the night of his death, they averred, "He was perfectly sober when at about 7 o'clock he left the house to go to the depot with his uncle." In fact, according to his brother-in-law, Sam Quintrall, Quinn had sworn that he was "never going to drink again. I'm going to save my money." A newspaper even noted that he refused a cigar offered to him by Quintrall, saying, "I'll never take another thing over a bar. That's the best way to quit—isn't it?"

However, later testimony suggested that Quinn never accompanied his uncle to the depot but rather visited several different saloons, ultimately ending up at Fitzgerald's at 630 B Street at California Street. Robert Hyndman was drinking with two young women there: Georgia Borden, age twenty-three, "known as [the married] Hyndman's sweetheart," and Mary Masten, a "youthful and incorrigible" seventeen-year-old girl recently released from the State Industrial School. Quinn arrived at Fitzgerald's at about 11:00 p.m., purchased a beer and walked to the wine rooms at the back of the saloon where Hyndman and his female companions were drinking. According to a report, Quinn flirted with Borden, saying to her, "Hello, Kid—how's tricks?" "That seemed to make Bob sore," Masten related. Hyndman soon became sick from drinking and left to vomit. Quinn reportedly sneered, "There's a guy who can't take two drinks of beer without getting drunk." An argument ensued, and the bartender, Fred Geiser, told Quinn to go home. Quinn refused, and a fight between him and Hyndman broke out, which Fitzgerald stopped. After this, Quinn departed. His body was found the next morning, lying facedown in the sandy bed of Cherry Creek, about 120 feet from Colfax Avenue toward Santa Fe Avenue.

PRINCIPALS AND A WITNESS IN THE KILLING OF QUINN.

JAMES QUINN. THE DEAD MAN.

ROBERT A. HYNDMAN,
Who Fought Quinn and Later Pursued Him.

WHERE THE BODY WAS FOUND

JOHN J. FITZGERALD.

Photomontage of the principal elements of the Hyndman case: victim James Quinn and suspect Robert Hyndman (both top); John J. Fitzgerald, saloonkeeper (bottom left); Fitzgerald saloon building and murder site near Cherry Creek.

The details of the following events were the subject of debate during the trial. Witnesses included saloon owner John Fitzgerald, Geiser and Borden. However, one of the most notable witnesses was Mary Masten. She stated that Hyndman followed Quinn out but quickly returned with a bleeding finger. Hyndman spoke to Geiser, telling him, "Come on and let us go look for that ---- [expletive deleted in original]." Masten also stated that Geiser then suggested that he and Hyndman take a walk. Another witness, a young man named August R. Allen, saw two men loudly talking after Quinn was supposed to have left the bar. Although Allen could not provide physical descriptions of the men, reports suggested that Allen's account provided support for Masten's testimony.

Yet another convincing witness was a street vendor, Charles Marshall, who was selling hot tamales in front of Fitzgerald's place. According to Marshall, Hyndman chased Quinn from the saloon and followed him down the street. Upon his return, Marshall noted that Hyndman said to him, "The ---- [expletive deleted in original] gave me a good chase, but I don't think he will run anymore." Shortly after returning to Fitzgerald's, Hyndman departed again with Geiser. Hyndman admitted to chasing Quinn away in the direction of Cherry Creek but that Quinn got away; Geiser supported the story.

The cause of Quinn's death was not precisely determined. "The presumption [was] that Quinn's pursuers overtook him, threw him down and suffocated him with a handkerchief," returning later to move his body to the bed of Cherry Creek with the intention of making the murder look like an accidental death. Hyndman was charged with murder; Geiser and Borden were charged as accessories before the fact. However, Hyndman's trial, which began on May 7, 1902, was anticlimactic. The testimony at the coroner's inquest was much more damaging to Hyndman than at his trial, and the *Denver Republican* noted that a "loss of memory makes many witnesses at the Hyndman trial valueless." Predictably, he was acquitted.

Chapter 2

Poison

The ready availability of arsenic and other poisons in the late nineteenth and early twentieth centuries resulted in a considerable number of related deaths, whether by suicide, homicide or accident (for example, a group of child poisonings in 1895 were the result of the distribution of free samples of a patent medicine called phengo-caffeine, which looked too much like candy). Probably the most famous poisoning case in Denver is the 1891 murder of Josephine Barnaby, who died after drinking from a bottle of poisoned whiskey she received in the mail. Barnaby was from Providence, Rhode Island, and visiting her friend Mrs. E.S. Worrell at the latter's home at 2226 Williams Street. Harvard-educated Dr. Thomas Thatcher Graves was found guilty of the crime; his motive was a large bequest in Barnaby's will. (A rash of additional poisonings in the same year in Denver—Annie Armstrong, the Hartung family and Joseph Ching—aroused additional concern in the city.) Notwithstanding the cases discussed here, the Pure Food and Drug Act of 1906 (21 U.S.C. 1 et seq.) required content and dosage labeling for certain drugs and thus mitigated some public anxiety regarding accidental poisonings.

THE COLE CHILDREN

"A deep, horrible mystery."

Family poisonings seemed to occur periodically, and investigators of the day were ill-prepared to separate death from natural causes (i.e., tainted food), accidental poisonings and deliberate murder. Moreover, even when poison was detected in an autopsy, proving exclusive control over the means of administration was nearly impossible. An early example is the death of Emelie Cole (aka Emilie), age three, and William Cole, age five, by strychnine poisoning on October 6, 1871. The children's mother, Catherine Miller, had left them in the care of Helen "Nellie" Conran, a neighbor, on September 24. Miller went to Wyoming to join her husband, who had left Denver after being implicated in a case of lumber theft.

Both Miller and Conran lived near the home of Johanna Bottig, a washerwoman from Germany with two daughters of her own. On the morning of the murder, Conran left the Cole children in the care of Bottig when she went to run errands. The children were at Bottig's residence on G Street below Wewatta when Bottig gave them pieces of jelly cake and a pear. They ate part of the cake but spit it out, claiming that it tasted "nasty." Within fifteen minutes, both children began to vomit and spasm.

Two local doctors were called, but Emelie died soon after they arrived. The doctors determined that the cause was the cake—crystalized strychnine was strewn over the top and between the layers. William was given an antidote. It appeared that he was recovering, but then he took a turn for the worse and died that evening. Bottig was arrested. Four other parties were taken into custody: Conran; Bottig's daughter, Louisa, age fourteen; and two "colored" men—James Boyce, who had previously boarded at Bottig's house, and Arthur Anderson, who brought his washing to Bottig. Conran was released that evening.

The coroner's jury heard testimony on the deaths of the two children beginning on October 7, 1871. According to her testimony, Bottig had found the cake and pears left on her table, located under a window with some broken panes. She stated, "People were in the habit of putting things on the table during our absence, especially dirty linen for us to wash." On Friday, seeing the children of Mrs. Miller playing about, she remembered the cake, got it and gave them portions of it to eat. She also noted that both her children ate portions of the cake and complained of the taste but did not become seriously ill. Bottig and others, including the local baker, testified that Jim Boyce and another black man had earlier come by the bakery and purchased the same cake that the children ate. Boyce and Anderson both stoutly denied bringing the cake to Bottig's house.

Another focal point of the trial was the enmity between Miller and Bottig. A number of witnesses testified that the women disliked each other and that there had been quarrels between them for some time (Bottig cited her own refusal to provide a character witness to Miller's husband as the starting point in their feud). Louisa attempted to place the blame on Boyce, stating that he had warned her not to eat the cake. The coroner's jury found that the poison was feloniously administered to the children by Bottig, Boyce and Anderson and that Louisa was an accessory.

However, the case stalled there. Bottig and Louisa were never indicted; there was no substantial evidence to convict Bottig, and she was released from police custody. Both Royce and Anderson were acquitted on October 29, 1871. As the *Central City Register* commented, the case was "still a deep, horrible mystery."

EMILY WITTER

"I would sooner give him up to God than that other woman."

The July 3, 1887 murder of John A. Witter, age thirty-eight, president of Percheron-Norman Horse Company and prominent Denverite, by his wife, Emily O. Witter (née Marble), age thirty-seven, in their home at South Eleventh and Fourteenth Avenues, was another sensational case. Emily and John Witter were Denver pioneers, arriving in the city in the early 1870s; John worked in the cattle business and was very successful.

Emily Witter.

It was initially thought that John Witter had passed away due to stomach cancer; he had been ill for several months. However, Emily became a suspect after a nurse attendant said that she had seen Emily adding a powder to John's milk. Chemical analyses found arsenic in the stomach and liver of the deceased. Emily was arrested and charged with several counts related to specific instances of administering poison to John in milk or "beef peptinoids." Bail was set at $10,000. Since the Witter fortune was estimated at $1,000,000, many citizens were more than willing to stand as sureties for her.

Her trial began on February 27, 1888. From the start, a conviction was not expected. The *National Police Gazette* picked up the story: "Will Mrs. Witter be convicted? The general belief is that she will not. No one in Denver for a moment would uphold any one in committing so terrible a crime as poisoning, but that Mrs. Witter suffered many wrongs and indignities the public knew, even before these later sensational developments were published."

During the trial, the prosecution used evidence from a state chemist to prove cause of death. The testimony of the nurse, Ida Whitaker, was damaging, as it showed Emily's involvement with John's care and her access to arsenic (not to mention her alleged statement that "I would sooner give him up to God than that other woman"). A druggist testified to several purchases of arsenic by Emily in May or June.

Other evidence indicated that John had been unfaithful to his wife with his young niece, Mrs. Hattie Hatten, age twenty-five. Testimony from Hiram Witter, John's brother, revealed that Hiram was not a beneficiary of his brother's will; instead, he was a trustee for money willed to Hattie Hatten. Moreover, the *News* noted, "It was shown that the whole family had reason to suspect John A. Witter's intimacy with his niece." Hiram's wife, Kate, testified, "I often reasoned with Mrs. Witter and tried to put the best face on the matter. She told me about John leaving her bed. She was frantic, at times seemed indignant, at other times broken down."

A number of witnesses stated that John was an inveterate taker of medicines, and some swore that they saw him take arsenic on several occasions. His physician, a Dr. Wheeler, stated as much: "The use of arsenical remedies is common with homeopaths. When Mr. Witter came to me I simply found a patient whom I thought needed arsenical remedies." Dr. Wheeler claimed that he tried these remedies on John for a time, but abandoned them when he did not obtain favorable results. This evidence would seem to have irreparably muddled the case, but the primary focus remained John's infidelity, as well as Emily's reluctance to hire a nurse during his illness from cancer. During the trial, she admitted that her husband did not trust her with his medicine and that she suspected that as soon as he was well, he would leave her. The defense counsel suggested in his closing argument that John had brought in nurse Whitaker to manufacture grounds for his divorce.

The *National Police Gazette*'s prediction came true. After Emily was on trial for nearly three weeks, on March 13, 1888, nearly a year after her husband's death, the jury returned a verdict of not guilty in the case against her after only two hours of deliberation. Spectators reportedly cheered wildly in approval.

Emily later married P.J. Thompson. He was subsequently charged with forging her name to a check. Upon her death at her home at 147 West Alameda Avenue on March 23, 1908, newspapers revisited her pioneer history but omitted any mention of the circumstances of John's death, the trial or Mr. Thompson. Emily left "a considerable estate" to her daughter. As one memorial put it, Emily Witter was known as a "home-loving woman, and while few enjoyed as extensive an acquaintance as she did, Mrs. Witter rarely went anywhere or mixed within the social life of the city."

THEODORE EHRHARDT

"If I die, I want you to have my husband arrested."

This case involves the December 19, 1909 murder of Josephine Ehrhardt (nicknamed "Tilly" by her family), age twenty-seven, after taking a powder purchased for her by her divorced husband, Theodore Ehrhardt, age thirty, a butcher by trade. The Ehrhardts, former residents of Topeka, Kansas, had taken a house at 2309 Curtis Street. The Ehrhardts had separated during the previous March, but according to the *Kansas City Star*, Theodore was

Josephine Ehrhardt (left) and Theodore Ehrhardt.

a frequent visitor at his ex-wife's home and provided continued financial support for their two children, who had remained with Josephine.

Although circumstances surrounding Josephine's death were initially unclear, a statement given by daughter Lillian ("Lilly"), age eight, on December 19, indicated her father's possible involvement in her mother's death. Lilly told the police that Theodore always bought medications for Josephine, and he gave her the box of powders in question. He reminded her later to "take one of them powders for your stomach trouble." In her statement to police, Lilly also mentioned that she had seen Theodore remove a powder, pretend to take it himself ("I don't think he did, though") and then wrap it in a piece of paper. At trial, she denied this.

After he left, Josephine ingested a powder, remarking on the bitter taste. She quickly fell ill and died the next morning. According to Dr. Noble Hamilton, who was called to attend to her, Josephine accused Theodore of having poisoned her. Another witness, fellow boarder Alfred Adair, stated that her dying words were, "If I die, I want you to have my husband arrested." This statement became an issue at trial, since it would only be admissible if she had expected her death to be imminent. The word "if" came in for considerable discussion; was she sure that she would die, or did it imply that she felt there was a chance she would recover?

The autopsy revealed that the cause of death was strychnine poisoning; the expected effect of ingesting it would be pain and convulsions within five

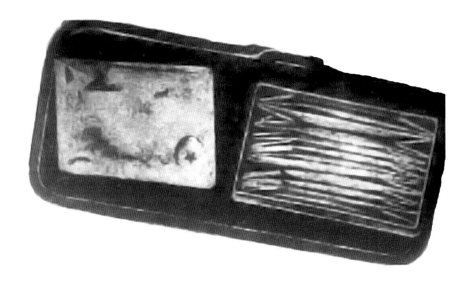

The medicinal powders that Theodore Ehrhardt gave to his wife.

to thirty minutes. Theodore was arrested on December 20 and charged with second-degree murder. The source of the poison was debated; some speculated that it may have been procured at a Littleton pharmacy at Nineteenth and Larimer, while others suggested that it might have come from Kansas City.

Theodore maintained that Josephine's death was the result of suicide. According to his testimony at trial, Josephine was never healthy, the marriage was unsuccessful because she did not care for him, her family all had consumption and her father died insane. (The latter arguments were rebutted by Ehrhardt's own plans to send his children to Josephine's sister in Lawrence, Kansas.) Moreover, he denied giving her the box of powders and claimed that Josephine deliberately committed suicide in a way that would cast suspicion on him.

Also arrested in connection with the case was Almira Lucretia "Lou" Gettinger, age thirty-two, Theodore's alleged mistress, who was living with him. Gettinger, who had met Theodore at a chili wagon in Kansas City where he was working at the time, denied any knowledge of the circumstances surrounding Josephine's death. Even so, she was willing to give her opinion: "Mrs. Ehrhardt committed suicide. Of this I am sure. As for knowing anything about the crime, it is preposterous on the part of the police to think that I do. Mr. Ehrhardt did not kill his wife. He loved her too much. It is true that he could not get along with her, and he may have been contemplating divorce, but I know he showed all kinds of affection for her."

He showed all kinds of affection for Gettinger as well. According to testimony from the police officer who arrested Theodore in a rooming house at 1921 Lawrence Street, he found them in Theodore's bed. Gettinger was also questioned about the arrest on the stand. She kept ducking the question, "You were in bed with Ehrhardt when he was arrested, weren't you?" with responses like, "We were in the same room, yes." The prosecutor persisted: "In the same bed, too, weren't you?" Gettinger finally replied, "Well, I had been."

Gettinger had been suspected of sending Theodore the strychnine from Kansas City, but no evidence was presented to support this and the charges against her were dropped. On April 8, 1910, Theodore Ehrhardt was convicted of second-degree murder in his wife's death and sentenced to thirty-five years in the penitentiary. However, in April 1911, the judgment was reversed on appeal on the grounds that the case should have been tried as first-degree murder, as required in all poison cases in Colorado at that time. Moreover, Lilly's testimony in court was substantially different from the written statement she gave the police. According to the *Post*, this meant that, while Ehrhardt would have to wait a new decision from the court regarding his sentence, he would not be sent to the penitentiary.

One interesting aspect to the public discussion surrounding the case was the supposedly unusual event of a man using poison to kill a woman. According to one report, "If Ehrhardt poisoned his wife he did a rather unusual thing for a man, since men, less emotional than women, less subtle, less fearful of making a mess; more thoughtful of escape and the future employ the quicker, colder method; they shoot, or stab or beat their victims and get out." Theodore married Gettinger in September 1911. After Gettinger's death in 1928, he was married a third time, to Dollie Warhover, in 1931.

ALVAH ESTABROOK

"One pancake would kill you if you could keep it down."

In 1926, Denver druggist and former cereal chemist Alvah W. Estabrook, age forty-seven, attempted to poison Kansas City Circuit Court judge Edward E. Porterfield. Estabrook, who operated a drugstore at 638 West Fourth Avenue at Galapago Street, was a former Kansas City resident. By 1925, his marriage to his wife Delaware (nicknamed "Della") had become strained; he particularly resented his wife's father, Cyrus Slater. A November 1925 letter from Della to a different juvenile court judge spells out some of the family problems:

> *Our first real trouble was in August, 1925. I remonstrated with him* [her husband] *over undue attentions paid to his stenographer. He threatened to leave me for this. In June 1924, he assaulted my father, who is a cripple, in front of our home for saying that he held kissing bees in his laboratory. After the assault, he pushed me out of the house, telling me that he was going for a shotgun and shells. The neighbors called the police. We had a property settlement in January, 1925, and I agreed to let the boy* [son Willard, age twelve] *remain with his father in Denver. I supposed this agreement would hold good until he obtained a divorce. His stenographer had followed him to Colorado.*

Judge Porterfield entered the story while these events were in progress. According to Porterfield, the Estabrook clan—husband, wife, son Willard and father-in-law—approached him informally in chambers in early July 1924. Porterfield related the discussion as follows:

I said to Mr. Slater, "What is the trouble?" I had never seen him before; he was a stranger to me. He said, "I was passing [Estabrook's] house…and he stepped out on the sidewalk and struck me with some instrument,"—I think he said, anyhow, he said, "He knocked me to the ground, unconscious." I said, "Mr. Estabrook, did you do that?" He said, "Yes." Then I asked Mrs. Estabrook what her trouble was and she told me a very harrowing story about him chasing her around the house with a gun…and I said, "Mr. Estabrook, did you do that?" He said, "Yes, sir; I did." Well, then I said, "You just get up and walk out. I don't want to talk to you at all, a man who will admit such cruelty and barbarity at all, I will not admit him here." He said, "Don't you want to hear my side?" I said "There couldn't be a side…Get up and go out."

Estabrook, angered, wrote the first of many threatening letters to Porterfield on October 11, accusing him of colluding with "one certain Masonic brother" (Cyrus Slater) to destroy his home and family. "The man is a slanderer and a liar and you have made yourself his assistant." Porterfield next encountered the Estabrooks at a custody hearing (date unspecified) in the juvenile court. Porterfield awarded custody of Willard to his mother and also took the opportunity to confront Estabrook about the October 11 letter. Estabrook retorted that "he wrote it and meant every word of it, and more; too; he said it in a very impudent manner." Then, when leaving the courtroom, Estabrook (probably deliberately) "sort of stumbled over his father-in-law." Porterfield admonished him, "You ought not to do that." He replied "in a very fierce way, 'Don't you talk to me that way.'" Porterfield promptly found him in contempt of court and ordered him to jail. Estabrook "got away from the sheriff on the way over" and actually served no time.

Estabrook, a tireless correspondent, wrote several more vituperative letters that were entered into evidence at his trial. He moved to Denver, where his sister lived, in late 1924; son Willard joined him. Estabrook opened his drugstore and took up residence in the rear of the building. From Denver, he wrote to Fidelity National Bank & Trust on November 13, explaining a late payment with these words: "This is late because of the illegal lying crazy acts of a judge in your city. This man lost his temper on the bench and by his criminal acts wrecked my family [and] sentenced me to jail and the penitentiary without a trial…He is a dirty coward…This

Alvah Estabrook.

Judge is E.E. Porterfield." He sent a copy to Porterfield, appending the words, "Remember, 'Old Boy,' you have a dirty price to pay and I am going to collect it."

The divorce was granted on January 2, 1926. Adopted daughter Annabel remained with Della.

Estabrook and Della continued to bicker by mail over custody of Willard, her failure to send Estabrook his diploma and certificates and the acts of the "dirty criminal" Porterfield. On March 4, 1926, Estabrook wrote that "Old Porterfield recently sent me word that he was going to put me in the pen if it was his last act in life. During the coming summer I plan to give him the opportunity he desires."

On about April 17, 1926, the Porterfields received a package of pancake flour in the mail. It was labeled "sample" and had been mailed in Denver. Porterfield's wife, Julia, prepared pancakes using the flour on May 18; she, her husband, their son and the dog ate them, apparently detecting nothing suspicious in their flavor. Within a short time, all became ill. Porterfield contacted a physician, who administered an emetic to induce vomiting and removed the remains of the flour for analysis. The package had actually contained about two pounds of flour mixed with an ounce of arsenic. As a

Judge Edward E. Porterfield and wife, Julia.

health department chemist testified at Estabrook's trial, "one pancake would kill you if you could keep it down."

The postal element placed Estabrook's case under federal jurisdiction. At the direction of a post office inspector, Denver police arrested Estabrook at his store on May 28; a bottle of "arsenious acid," a typewriter and a package addressed to Cyrus Slater were taken into evidence at the same time.

Estabrook was tried in the U.S. District Court for the Western District of Missouri, charged with attempted murder and misuse of the postal system. He pleaded not guilty by reason of insanity; both his son and sister testified to his erratic behavior and obsession with Porterfield, and the defense argued that Estabrook previously had good standing within his community. He was found guilty and sentenced to fifteen years' imprisonment at the United States penitentiary at Leavenworth, Kansas. In 1935, his paranoid behavior led to his transfer to the discouragingly named United States Hospital for Defective Delinquents at Springfield, Missouri. This deprived him of the good-time credit he had earned at Leavenworth, and he pursued a petition for his release to the Eighth Circuit Court of Appeals (eventually denied in 1941).

VIRGIL MASSIE

"To my question as to why he did not call a doctor instead of calling me he made no answer."

Liquor control was adopted in Colorado in 1916, but the state still allowed the sale of medicinal alcohol; further, Wyoming was a "wet" state, and alcohol could easily be imported from there. With stricter national prohibition laws effective in 1920, bootlegging became an effective and easy way of making money.

Virgil Massie, age thirty, was a prohibition enforcement officer and a Lakewood resident in 1926. The title "prohibition enforcement officer" was an ambiguous and unofficial one (as one court decision noted, "there is no such office or employment"). Often it encompassed individuals who could be colloquially described as "thugs and blackmailers" or "snitches." There are indications that Massie fell into the questionable end of the spectrum. His enforcement activities appeared to be marginally productive at best, and he and his friends were regular and copious alcohol consumers. In court, his job was characterized as "going in and acquiring the friendship of a man, representing yourself to him as a friend, and then turning around and getting him to sell you liquor and turning him in."

Virgil and his wife, Katherine (née Rosenboom), age thirty-six, lived in Lakewood in Jefferson County. They were childless and appeared to have had a companionable but unromantic relationship. Virgil had a longstanding extramarital relationship with Mrs. Rene Divelbess (née Lorine Gardner), age forty-five, wife of a Navajo County, Arizona sheriff. Virgil took Rene with him on his business trips to visit speakeasies and buy illegal alcohol in Kit Carson County because he was investigating dance halls, and "you couldn't get in unless you brought your own partner." At his trial, friends would note a marked diminution of his attentions to Katherine and the many nights he spent away from home. Rene had taken an apartment in Denver, and he visited her frequently.

Virgil and Katherine Massie enjoying one of their festive picnics. Massie offered the photographs at trial as evidence of their happy marriage. *Colorado State Archives.*

On Sunday, January 31, 1926, Virgil and Katherine went on a pleasure trip with another couple, Andrew and Mary Roebke, and returned to their home at about 2:00 p.m. As reported by the Colorado Supreme Court opinion on Virgil's appeal, the evening was festive (note the recurrence of the word "whiskey"):

> *Whiskey was procured, the men drank, all dined at 3 p.m., and defendant, on pretense of business and over the protest of his wife, left at 4 p.m. Thereupon Mrs. Massie and the others attended a theater in Denver, returned home, dined and drank whiskey, and the friends left at 11:30 p.m. Upon his departure that afternoon, defendant repaired to the room of his mistress in a Denver hotel where together they drank whiskey, then dined out and parted at 11 p.m.... [Massie] says he reached home about midnight, found his wife*

in bed apparently drunk, took a drink himself, fired the furnace, threw into it an empty whiskey bottle, and went to bed with his wife. About 4 p.m. on Monday Mrs. Divelbess, in response to a telephone call, went to the Massie home. There she found defendant apparently very ill, lying in bed beside his dead wife. She called a doctor and later a nurse was summoned. Sufficient fire was found in the furnace to last for two hours and on top of it lay an uncorked whiskey bottle. The nurse and Mrs. Divelbess cared for defendant until Wednesday. The body of Mrs. Massie was taken to a Denver mortuary and later, accompanied by defendant, to her old home at Carthage, Illinois, where it was interred February 7. When defendant departed for Carthage he left Mrs. Divelbess in charge of his home, first having made the necessary arrangements, by cash and credit, for her maintenance and support there. He returned in a few days and took up his abode with her.

The first physician on the scene was Dr. Edward Martin, an osteopath contacted by Rene Divelbess. He certified Katherine's death as a result of cerebral hemorrhage. Virgil made a point of verifying with him that an osteopath's certification was acceptable to an insurance company. However, this was not the end of the story. Katherine's relatives were suspicious and disturbed by Virgil's demeanor at the Illinois funeral, and they hired the Pinkerton Detective Agency to investigate. Katherine's body was disinterred in early March, and an autopsy revealed arsenical poisoning. Both Virgil and Rene were charged with murder.

Massie's case was tried in Adams County after a change of venue and began on May 10, 1926. Massie proved to be an unsympathetic witness, often appearing to be intentionally obtuse or sarcastic. Prosecutor and defense counsel went at the case full force, both having to be cautioned for loud and angry interrogations of witnesses, aggressive gesticulations and pejorative references (for example, Rene was referred to as Virgil's "paramour," and his initial relations with her as "picking her up"). No holds were barred. Virgil's counsel offered to prove that Katherine had been diagnosed with vaginal warts in September 1925 and became morose and suicidal, fearing that she had contracted syphilis. According to Virgil, Katherine had stated that if this were the case, "she would need no doctor to care for her, but rather an undertaker." This evidence was excluded, but it probably contributed to the prosecutor's obvious distaste for Virgil. He referred to the defendant as a "despicable coward" and an "out and out hypocrite."

Rene Divelbess was not very helpful on the stand. She unconvincingly portrayed her relationship with Virgil as a simple friendship. Her visit to the

Massie home on February 1 was in response to a 2:00 p.m. telephone call from Virgil; he was sick, his wife was home and he wanted her to come to the house, but not until 4:00 p.m. When she arrived, Katherine was dead and Virgil told her that he did not know when she died:

> *To my question as to why he did not call a doctor instead of calling me he made no answer. He told me there were no neighbors at home who could be called (which was untrue) and thereafter when I proposed calling a doctor he twice protested. I did call Dr. Martin by telephone. He was slow in coming and I called him the second time. After his arrival defendant asked me not to tell him that he had "phoned me." I asked him why he told me not to come until four o'clock. He said because he did not wish to frighten me. Thereafter I talked with him many times about what I should say if I were arrested.*

The other woman: Rene Divelbess.

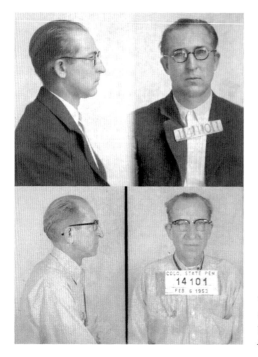

Virgil Massie in prison, upon conviction in 1926, and twenty-nine years later in 1955. *Colorado State Archives.*

The jury members found him guilty in the first degree and fixed the penalty at life imprisonment. His motion for a new trial was overruled. Massie filed an unsuccessful appeal in 1927 based on the omission of the alleged "loathsome disease" evidence related to Katherine, but the appellate court ruled that the exclusion was proper. The prosecutor's remarks represented a second ground of appeal, but the court was again unimpressed:

> *The evidence afforded ample justification for the language complained of. It was unfortunate for defendant that at so critical a moment in his life his character and conduct were so interwoven with the transaction under investigation that they could not be ignored, and so reprehensible, and even criminal, as to testify against him in tones which required no emphasis from the tongue of the district attorney to carry into the jury box. But this record was written by defendant himself and was properly in evidence. In reading it to the jury no duty devolved upon the prosecutor to find pretty names for ugly deeds.*

Virgil remained in prison and grew old there, as witnessed by his mug shots over the years. As for Rene Divelbess, according to the 1930 census, she was back in Holbrook, Arizona, with her husband, Louis Daniel "Dan" Divelbess.

Chapter 3

"Abuse and Vilification"

A 2006 study of intimate homicide in Denver and New York City from 1880 to 1920 by Carolyn B. Ramsey looked at the treatment of male and female perpetrators in "intimate violence" cases. In contrast to the view that male violence, unlike female violence, was minimized or excused by the courts, Ramsey concluded that courts and juries tacitly recognized a "battered woman's defense" (which did not formally exist during the time period). In short, women were able to claim that they were defending themselves against abuse or avenging infidelity in the same way that men traditionally used the heat of passion and self-defense for justification or excuse.

HELEN SCHMIDLAP

"More than a self-respecting woman would tolerate."

The first of many similar Denver cases of this kind was the July 9, 1905 murder of William Schmidlap, age forty-four, traveling salesman, by his wife, Helen Schmidlap, age thirty-nine. This case was, according to journalists, "one of the most sensational tragedies that ever took place in Denver." Helen (née Goodrich) was the former wife of Albert Ezekiel, a U.S. marshal, with whom she had two young sons. While married to Ezekiel, she met William, then a drug salesman for the Davis-Bridaham Drug Company, in Colorado Springs. William soon broke off his engagement to another woman, and Helen asked her husband for a divorce. William and Helen married as soon as the divorce was final, in February 1903.

Helen Schmidlap.

The romance was soon over. William lost his job at Davis-Bridaham and was nearly out of employment options: "His inability to remain sober drove him from one position to another until recently he had made but a meager and intermittent living traveling for the Colorado Cigar Company." William's inebriation, which might have been tolerable to Helen if he were earning income, became a source of contention. The couple argued frequently, and according to Helen, William often mistreated and abused her. The final horror was when he suggested that she lead a life of shame: "You are young and pretty, and to such money comes easy." While their divorce had not yet been granted, the Schmidlaps separated, and Helen left Denver for Los Angeles with her children. (As the *Post* reported from William's funeral, "There was but one opinion among all of the men who knew him in his lifetime: 'Billy was his own enemy.'")

The circumstances of the murder as related during the trial were comparatively straightforward. After about a year of estrangement, Helen "became despondent because of his cruelty, dissipation and refusal to support her." She testified that she "first decided to asphyxiate herself and children but thought better of this step and resolved first to kill her husband." Upon returning to Denver, she confronted her husband at the Clarendon rooming house, located at 1517 Arapahoe Street, carrying a .30 caliber revolver in her handbag. She asked him why he had disgraced and abused her and why he had tried to make her prostitute herself. His only reply was that he had done it because she was "mutty." He noticed her handbag and asked her what was in it, to which she replied that she had a gun.

According to Helen, he then "picked [the handbag] up and threw it on the bed. I was sitting on a chair. Then he remarked in a casual way: 'What are you going to do about it?' I replied: 'Unless you brace up and take care of me and the children, I am going to kill you.' Without hesitation he answered: 'Oh, no, you won't; I'll bump us both off.'" An argument and a struggle for the gun ensued, and she shot him three times. Helen stated that she left the room, came across the landlady and a policeman and handed over both herself and the gun to police custody.

Helen was initially charged with murder in the first degree on the recommendation of the coroner, to which her defenses were self-defense and insanity. Much was made of her appearance ("She is a remarkably beautiful blonde"; "Mrs. Schmidlap enjoys the distinction of being the most beautiful woman ever lodged in the city jail"; and she was "a woman of innate refinement"); the emotional visits of sons Louis, age seven, and Marcus, age five, to the jail; and the "shattering of all her ideals" that came about when William mistreated her.

Her first husband, Albert Ezekiel, came to Helen's defense, though rumors of a remarriage were so pervasive that he issued a statement to contradict them. "I am only staying by my boys. I do not want a stain over their heads. I wouldn't live with Lena [Helen's nickname] one moment if she was clear, for I cannot tell what she would do when she was under an insane spell." Helen appeared "very much annoyed" when the subject of Ezekiel came up.

Her trial began on October 17, 1905. News stories claimed that she was extremely stressed by the proceedings (which took place at the West Side Court) and had attempted to hang herself in her jail cell on July 15. Ezekiel testified on her behalf, describing his placid married life with Helen until William (as defense counsel put it) "came into the household with black heart and mind." Evidence of hereditary insanity in Helen's family was also presented. The members of the jury at Helen's first trial were unable to reach a verdict, resulting in a mistrial on October 26. According to the foreman, the last ballot was eight for acquittal and four for conviction.

A second trial was held at the beginning of the following year, although reporters noted that it was difficult to secure suitable members for the jury because of the widespread knowledge and public interest in the case. The second trial received less extensive coverage, though public and media interest remained in its potential outcome. Helen had altered her account of the shooting slightly in her conversations with reporters, emphasizing that she had always carried a revolver with her, that William had threatened to shoot her and that she had fired in self-defense. This was in direct contradiction to a newsboy witness who overheard a woman's voice in the room saying, "Brace up or I'll kill you. I came all the way from California to do it, and

I will." She did not take the stand at this trial, and Ezekiel, unexpectedly, did not testify. New evidence concerned Helen's frequent visits to saloons and the somewhat dubious insinuation that she had encouraged and abetted William's drinking.

Ultimately, Helen was found not guilty in the murder of her husband on February 6, 1906, much to the excitement of the audience in the courtroom, many of whom were anxious to shake her hand as she left. Her published statement following her acquittal was as follows (emphasis in original):

> *If I am guilty of any crime it has been that I have not tamely submitted to abuse and vilification from a drunken and abandoned husband that no self-respecting woman would tolerate. Had I done so I would not have been my father's child! I REVERSED THE USUAL RULE and while admitting the necessity is a terrible one, yet I have never felt, nor do I now feel that under the circumstances I would not do the same thing again. My revolver spoke for me and mine and for all that a wife holds near and sacred.*

It should also be noted that the verdict in the Schmidlap case was subjected to some criticism by the presiding judge, Samuel Carpenter, who stated that the outcome of the trial was "not in accord with his idea of justice." The jurors, naturally, expressed great displeasure in this comment.

Immediately after the trial, there were reports that Helen had been offered a vaudeville role, that she had twenty offers of marriage or that her health was poor and she intended to retire to her home state of Arizona. She was quoted as saying that Christian Science had come into her life while she was in jail and that "it has made a great change in my condition of thought."

Six months after the conclusion of the trial, despite her proclaimed wishes to fade from public attention, Helen was implicated in a suit for divorce filed by Matilda Kuppinger against her husband, charging him with infidelity. Following this incident, Helen was once again brought into the public eye by her former in-laws. The wife of William's brother, Cale, claimed that she was "snubbed and insulted" on a trip to California because "I was mistaken for that woman. On the train people sneered at me, made ugly remarks… people only knew I was Mrs. Schmidlap of Denver and they took it for granted I was she."

CARMELINA FIORINO

"She was chaste once. She was innocent, pure and devoted, and her ruin was accomplished by this man."

Denver's population grew by 275 percent between 1880 and 1900 (from 35,629 to 133,859) and by 115 percent between 1900 and 1930 (from 133,859 to 287,861). In the process, it also became more ethnically diverse. The city's "Little Italy" was located roughly between Forty-sixth and Thirty-seventh Avenues on the north and south and Broadway and Zuni Street on the east and west. Many of the immigrants there retained close family ties with their native villages, and the male-to-female ratio was much higher than in eastern cities. In other words, it was a community of families.

However, this is not to say that the relocation was painless. Historian Janet Worrell, among others, has noted that Denver's Italian community offered women increased opportunities as wage earners outside the home. This undoubtedly exposed them to a greater sphere of activity and growing expectations. The restrictive gender roles that held sway in Italy did not transfer smoothly to Denver, and some domestic violence cases reflect the stress of the transition.

Several of these involved "child brides." Two cases were particularly notorious. On May 15, 1906, the naked body of Rosa Composte (née Serico or Sario), age fourteen, was found in her "miserable hovel" of a home at 2437 Central Court; her husband, George, age somewhere between twenty-five and thirty, had killed her with a hatchet and then attempted to decapitate her with a razor. The couple had married six months earlier in San Francisco.

George Composte (aka Comperio, Voleso or George Wallace), a laborer, had reportedly deserted a first wife in New York. The woman turned up in California in search of him, and this prompted George and Rosa to leave for Denver. Rosa was miserable in the marriage. A friend told the story as follows: "George treated Rosa shamefully. She was young and only put on long dresses when she married. She liked to play with the children in the neighborhood and George used to beat her for that. She was young and did not know how to cook and do other things around the house, and he beat her unmercifully for that."

Later the same year, Carmelina Fiorino (née Nigro; aka Carmella, Carmelia, Maria Carmelina, Cornelia or many other variations) became a short-term media celebrity when she shot and killed her husband, Gaetano. Both were from Grimaldi in Calabria, Italy. Carmelina arrived in the

Gaetano and Carmelina Fiorino, the wedding photograph.

United States in 1904 and was married to Gaetano in Denver in April 1905 when she was sixteen years old. Some sources referred to her as his mistress. Gaetano had left a wife and three children behind in Italy, so the marriage was bigamous at best. The Fiorinos lived at 2057 Delgany Street, where the murder took place on August 6, 1906.

Gaetano, age forty-five, was seated at the kitchen table one day, writing a letter. He had announced his intention of informing her relatives of Carmelina's bad conduct and the dishonor she had brought to his name. This may or may not have had severe consequences. As the *Post* soberly reported, "The unwritten law of concubinage provides that [her] brother should come to this country and by torture or the stiletto end the domestic discord." The letter in question read (as translated):

> *Dear Brother-in-Law Celestino—These few lines I write to let you know about your sister Carmelina. I would like her to be good. She never appears to be good to me. Her face shows she is bad. I can say nothing to her. She goes to the door and solicits men who pass. She said she could make her living by her own wits. I believe she has some bad intentions in her head. She scorns her husband. I never called her a name. She never cared for me. She looked to other men for her food. She said all the time that she had the best of me.*

The letter remained unfinished. Carmelina approached Gaetano from behind and fired two shots from a revolver, one of which entered the back of his head.

Gaetano died the next day. His deathbed statement said that he had been writing the letter to "scare" her, but it also included the admissions that "I have beat her a couple of times" and "I had a fight with her last night before she shot me." Carmelina was arrested immediately upon the arrival of the police and charged with murder. Her defense was Gaetano's physical abuse; he had been arrested for beating Carmelina before, in one instance on Easter Sunday. She had fled the marriage earlier, leaving with another man to reside in Leadville, and apparently had returned to Gaetano under duress.

While Carmelina received some sympathetic coverage in local newspapers, the Italian community appeared to have closed ranks against her. The man for whom Carmelina allegedly left Gaetano in August 1905, one Gennaro Anselmo ("a former sweetheart"), could not be located by the prosecution and was reputedly in hiding. Several friends and relatives of Gaetano's testified that Carmelina stated that her husband was "too old," that she did not love him and that she had engaged in licentious conduct with other men during her stay in Leadville. She lived with a man named Michaelo Parnetti in Leadville, but at least one witness appeared to think of them as relatives rather than as a couple in an intimate relationship. The house they occupied had two bedrooms, and Carmelina earned money by taking in washing. According to her testimony at trial, she was arrested in Leadville (charges unspecified) and told that if she did not return to her husband, she would be sentenced to eighteen years in prison. Clearly she had a minimal understanding of her alleged offense or the potential penalty, but she rejoined Gaetano in Denver nonetheless.

During the trial, which began on October 8, 1906, Carmelina's demeanor was pleasant and cheerful, which led reporters to speculate that she was "like a child, without any appreciation of the gravity of the situation." She reputedly spoke little English, and this is borne out by the way reporters occasionally chose to transcribe her comments in a sort of pidgin English. Newspapers included numerous photographs of her, apparently taken by her youth, vivacity and good looks. Often the reporters themselves seemed to lose track of the gravity of the situation as well; one enthused, "Carmelina's face is a study. It is pretty and not pretty, delicate and coarse, good and bad, and all things with each change of feeling. The high cheek bones and ignorant expression indicate the peasant girl; the mouth at times is as hard as that of a middle-aged woman of the lower world, the nose that of a coquette. But the artist must admire the low, broad brow; the beautiful, wide-apart, expressive eyes, and the mouth, with its drawn-in under lip, is the mouth Rosetti loved to paint in portrait and in verse."

Indeed, the same article refers to Carmelina as an "enigma," and these kinds of comments reflect the unease that her case created. She was very

Carmelina Fiorino, before and after conviction. *Colorado State Archives (image at right).*

young and had been forced into a marriage with a much older, abusive man, factors pleading in her favor. On the other hand, she was not a "lady," and even her supporters could not make a case for her delicate and outraged sensibilities. Unlike Gertrude Patterson and Stella Smith (discussed later), she would stay ruined. Carmelina's attorney referred to her moral character in his closing argument:

> *She was chaste once. She was innocent, pure and devoted, and her ruin was accomplished by this man Fiorino…She was a stranger in a strange land; she had no place of refuge, no confidant, and this man could tell her whatever he had a mind to, and she had to believe him…They would tell you that he was joking when he brandished a revolver about the head of this little girl, and held before her continually the fate of Rosa Composto, who was murdered while she slept.*

Five hours of jury deliberation brought back a verdict. Carmelina was found guilty of voluntary manslaughter on October 12, which provided for a sentence in the range of one to ten years in the state penitentiary. She was, in fact, sentenced to two to three years in prison on October 27. In February

1907, Carmelina was visited in prison at Canon City by a female reporter for the *Post*, who commented on her amiable temperament: "She chattered and talked and laughed about how pleasant it was there. 'Everybody like me here—matron like me, good people, not like in my house, Denver,' and she shrugged her shoulders."

LOTTIE WEBB

"He had no right to treat me as he did and then desert me for another girl."

On June 17, 1909, Lottie Webb (aka Pereault), age twenty-five, shot and killed Horace Pereault, age twenty-eight, at their residence at 1839 Lawrence Street after a quarrel. Both parties were African American. Horace, a porter at the Hippodrome on Sixteenth Street, had brought Lottie to Denver from Dallas, Texas; she was known as his wife. The day before the crime, Horace went to a picnic at Locust Grove with Josephine Carroll, age fifteen. Lottie learned of this and promptly went to a pawnshop at 1942 Larimer. She bought a revolver and told Horace's friends that she would kill him the next time she saw him. When Horace heard of this, he came to the house at Lawrence Street. Lottie, true to her word, shot him three times and then went to police headquarters and turned herself in.

Lottie Webb Pereault.

Interviewed by the *Republican* the next day, Lottie admitted that she would have killed Josephine as well if she had encountered her. She summarized her grievances against Horace as follows: "I would be telling a lie if I said that I was sorry that Pereault is dead. He made me suffer

49

and he deserved all he got. I had lived with him for over twelve years and during all that time I supported him. He put me in a crib at 1429 Twenty-first street and made me turn over to him all the money I earned…I considered him my husband and he had no right to treat me as he did and then desert me for another girl."

Lottie was a very small woman (four feet, ten and three-fourths inches and ninety-five pounds). She did not, however, claim that Horace had physically threatened her. She was sentenced to six to eight years for voluntary manslaughter. In light of the other cases discussed here, it is impossible not to wonder if Lottie's forthrightness doomed her to conviction.

GERTRUDE PATTERSON

"If ever there was a woman who is a demon on earth in her home and then makes outsiders believe she is maltreated terribly, it is her."

Gertrude Patterson.

No case was more heavily reported than the September 25, 1911 murder of Charles Patterson, age twenty-six, by his wife, Gertrude Gibson Patterson (aka Gertrude Knight or Birdie Knight), age thirty. This case attracted national attention because of Gertrude's beauty, the carefully framed dramatic narratives presented during the trial and the division of public opinion on the matter of the defendant's guilt.

The events immediately preceding the murder were as follows. Gertrude and a young man named George W. Strain were sitting on the porch at Gertrude's bungalow at 1008 Steele Street. He had been in the habit of visiting Gertrude and had brought a gun with him since she had told him that her husband had a violent temper. Charles Patterson and a friend appeared at the house unexpectedly. Strain found his manner threatening, so he drew the revolver and ordered Charles to leave. After he was gone, Gertrude asked him if he could leave the gun with her for her protection.

On September 25, 1911, Gertrude encountered Charles, who was suffering from tuberculosis, at the Agnes Phipps Memorial Sanitarium. They walked down the street together to one of the more isolated areas in the vicinity, near the E.B. Hendrie Mansion at 7020 East Twelfth Avenue (later known as the Von Richthofen Castle). There Gertrude shot Charles. A witness, A.B. Shugart, heard the shot and saw Charles on his hands and knees. Gertrude then shot him a second time, dropped the revolver and ran through the gate of the Hendrie Mansion. Shugart followed Gertrude and asked her who the injured man was. "He is my husband and he wronged me," she replied.

Gertrude offered several accounts of the homicide. First, she stated that Charles had shot himself. Next, she said that they had struggled for the gun after arguing about an alienation of affection suit that he was pressing against her former companion, the wealthy Chicago businessman Emil W. Strouss, age fifty. At trial, she said that Charles had demanded money from her and wanted her to deed the bungalow to him and then said, "You will sign or I'll choke the life out of you." He grabbed her by the throat, struck her in the face, knocked her to the ground and kicked her. She managed to pull out the revolver and shoot him. The coroner's report indicates that Charles was shot from the back.

An assortment of fanciful anecdotes began to surround Gertrude early in the case, assisted by her less-than-candid interviews with the press. What we might call the "folktale" of Gertrude Patterson began in small-town Illinois. The young Gertrude Gibson was "the most attractive of the village girls, [and her] ambition soared above the town's life," noted the *Wilkes-Barre Times*. At some unidentified location, the sixteen-year-old met Emil W. Strouss, senior partner in the Chicago clothing manufacturing firm of Strouss, Eisendrath & Company. (There are no available photographs of Strouss, but a news article described him, fairly or not, as "extremely unattractive.") Strouss's intentions were entirely honorable. As Gertrude noted, "After many conferences with my people he finally took me to Paris, where he provided me with a tutor, arranged for my taking music lessons, and [he] departed almost immediately. I was very happy and worked hard at my studies as I wanted him to be proud of his future wife," according to the *New York Times*. When she returned to the United States, she was commonly introduced as his wife, but their relationship was, allegedly, unsatisfactory to her.

Census records tell a different story. In 1900, Gertrude, age eighteen, and her sister, Myrtle, age nineteen, were residents of Chestnut Street in St. Louis, Missouri. Both are listed as "house girls"; lest the euphemism go unrecognized, the census taker noted "House of Ill Fame" and "prostitutes" on the page. This is also evidenced in the demographics of the surrounding dwellings, which were populated by unrelated female "house girls" almost exclusively. Did the Parisian trip ever happen? There are no passport applications in any combination of Gertrude's names, and Strouss, who did make many trips abroad, is invariably listed as traveling alone. The story explains Gertrude's missing teenage years, but it is based on her word alone. This is frequently the case with her accounts, and it may be a combination of self-mythologizing and newspaper reporters' desire for a dramatic story.

Gertrude's relationship with Strouss probably was unsatisfying, because in the summer of 1908, she met the young, handsome and athletic Charles Patterson in Chicago. The two began a romance, and they were married on a trip to California. Gertrude had allegedly broken with Strouss. When the couple returned to Chicago, their troubles began. Both sides claimed that they had been abused or betrayed by the other. Charles was unhappy about Gertrude's relationship with Strouss. At trial, Gertrude claimed that Charles extracted money from Strouss for marrying her and later forced her to resume her relationship with Strouss for money: "He sold me to Strouss: Strouss gave him $1,500 to keep me as long as he wished…more than that, at other times

Left to right: Myrtle Farnham, Gertrude's sister; Charles Patterson, victim; and George Strain, Gertrude's admirer and provider of the gun.

my husband insisted upon my going to Strouss for money and he knew what that meant to me. He beat me, and he insisted upon my being bad."

Four months after the marriage, according to Gertrude, she and Strouss went on a European trip for several months. He could not speak French, and she assisted him in making purchases. Also in 1908, Charles developed pneumonia, followed by tuberculosis, and the couple moved from Chicago to Denver to seek treatment. Charles could not work and required costly medical treatment. Gertrude was forced to mortgage her stocks and bonds "so her husband could be comfortable…[she] had nursed him during the siege of pneumonia until her own health had given way and after all this, he 'choked me, spat in my face and treated me like a dog.'" She also claimed that "from the time I moved to Steele Street I can't even bear to think about it, let alone write. It's one horrible nightmare of beatings and kicks. He twisted my arms. What a strange thing it is that some people are born to trouble as the birds to fly."

Ultimately, Charles entered the sanitarium for treatment, and she acquired an apartment nearby so that she could help care for him. However, despite her attempts to nurse him back to health, "Things were no better between them and his treatment of her was as cruel as ever. At the advice of a lawyer she applied for a divorce from him."

The prosecution in the Patterson case presented a very different image of Gertrude and her relationship to her deceased husband. She had a long history of deceiving Charles. The trip to Europe with Strouss in 1909 was, in fact, of her own volition and without her husband's knowledge. The prosecution claimed that Patterson believed that his wife was simply visiting family in St. Louis (which, perhaps, she was, as Strouss claimed that he had been in Europe but "was not accompanied by a Mrs. Patterson nor any other woman"). Charles's mother denied the allegation that he had "sold" Gertrude and offered evidence to show that she sent half of her teacher's salary to the Pattersons each month; moreover, Mrs. Patterson stated that she herself had paid all of his medical expenses. Moreover, Charles was so weakened by tuberculosis that he weighed 110 pounds; he was unlikely to have the stamina to be physically abusive.

Patterson wrote in his diary, "If ever there was a woman who is a demon on earth in her home and then makes outsiders believe she is maltreated terribly, it is her; the lies she tells and the way she can purr, and work on people's feelings surely makes outsiders believe me a devil, but such is not the case…so God help me, I have been as true in thought, word and deed to that woman I married and loved as it was possible for God to make a man be." Other passages, earlier in the relationship, showed his affection for Gertrude and a more companionable relationship. Yet it should be noted that these feelings were clearly not present in September 1911. Gertrude had filed for divorce in Denver on September 1. Charles responded on September 20 with an alienation of affection suit against Strouss for the sum of $25,000.

Gertrude's trial began on November 20. She was charged with murder. Most of the reports regarding the trial focus on the evidence presented and the testimonials delivered in court, paying particular attention to the lurid retellings of Patterson's life story and the dramatic arc of her relationship with her deceased husband. Far less attention was paid in the papers to the legal aspects of the trial or the arguments being made in court. However, some reports did make note of the composition of the jury "of comparatively young men" and speculated that its members were enamored of Gertrude's beauty. Regardless, Gertrude was acquitted on November 29. She was greeted by a cheering crowd as she left the courtroom. Detective Sam Howe made three separate notations in his "murder book" regarding his opinion of the case: "Rotten verdict—condemned by all good people," "Rotten" and "Jury acquittal—the worst ever."

Following the trial, Gertrude left Denver for Chicago, saying that after she visited her father there, she would visit family in Oregon. However, her path becomes increasingly difficult to follow after this point. Reportedly, she was using her maiden name. According to one story in the *News*, she was installed in a "palatial villa" in Fontainebleau, France, by Strouss, where she planned to write two autobiographical books (entitled, respectively, *The Flames of Love* and *The Bachelor*). Neither book appears to have seen the light of day, and the entire story has the ring of Gertrude's invention. It was, of course, unverifiable.

In 1912, a rumor arose that she was a passenger on the *Titanic*, though this was the result of confusion between Emil Strouss—not on the ship—and actual passengers Isidor Strauss and wife. In November 1913, an article in the paper stated that she was leaving Fontainebleau, but there was no specific mention of her next destination. Emil Strouss died in March 1930, still unmarried.

STELLA SMITH

"Do the jelly wobble on your hands and knees."

Another high-profile case centered on the January 13, 1917 murder of John Lawrence Smith, age thirty-one, by his estranged wife, Stella Moore Smith, age forty-one, an elegant Denver socialite. Stella Smith (née Newton) was the former wife of William A. Moore, a prominent Denver attorney. She was also the stepdaughter of Alfred Britton, a wealthy oil magnate. Stella and Moore had one daughter, Mildred, in 1904. John Lawrence Smith was hired as a chauffeur for Stella's father, with whom the Moores were then living. A romance between Stella and Smith, "a good-looking youth with the plausible way which characterizes so many of his kind," blossomed, and she and Moore were divorced in October 1912. Moore was given sole custody of Mildred. Smith and Stella married in March 1914.

Smith remains the enigma in the case. He had been married before and had a son, Herbert, age seven. It seems that little information was ever elicited about his friends, previous employers or background. In Stella's view, she quickly learned that she had married "a drunken degenerate…and the life she was compelled to lead thereafter was filled with horrors more dreadful to her sensitive nature…than even the prospects of forfeiting her life on the gallows." In addition, he was a financial drain on Stella, who claimed that he did not work and that she had given him money that he wasted in "fast living." In December 1916, she negotiated an arrangement with Moore to regain custody of Mildred, now age twelve, provided that Smith was not allowed to visit her home at 4040 Mountview Boulevard. Smith moved to the Oxford Hotel. When he and Stella were in Denver, he remained there, but they traveled together and had, in fact, just returned from two weeks in Niagara Falls. (To complicate matters further, Moore lived in the house when

Photomontage of the principals in the Smith case: victim John Lawrence Smith (left); the accused, Stella Moore Smith (right); and Stella's ex-husband, William A. Moore (below).

the Smiths were away and stayed at the Tremont Hotel when they were in town.) One would expect this revolving arrangement to be unsatisfactory, and on the day of the crime, Smith came to the Mountview house at 2:00 a.m. and demanded entry.

Stella's account of the period between 2:00 a.m. and 5:30 a.m. was as follows. She and Smith quarreled loudly about her request for a divorce. The servants became alarmed and summoned Moore to come and pick up Mildred. Moore arrived in a cab, and a servant brought Mildred out to him because Smith would not allow Stella to go. As Moore left, Smith threatened to shoot him through the window, but Stella bumped him so that he could not aim. During the trial, Moore said, "I suppose I ought to have killed Smith myself, but I had not the heart to do it."

After Moore's departure, the events played out in Stella's bedroom. Smith forced her to drink whiskey. Then he "commanded me to take off every stitch I had on and 'do the jelly wobble on your hands and knees around that chair.'" As Stella later related, "I don't know what a jelly wobble is, but I knew he meant for me to crawl around that chair on my hands and knees. He said I had to do what he told me to." He tore off Stella's clothes, continued to force her to drink whiskey, cursed at her and slapped and pinched her. At one point, when Smith left the room, Stella removed a pistol from a dresser drawer and hid it under a pillow.

Smith went in the bathroom to get some water. When he returned, Stella pulled out the gun, a .22-caliber pistol, and shot him in the head. "I didn't think that he was badly injured, and that he would get his own gun and kill me, so I jumped up and ran to the telephone table, where he had left the weapon. Then I ran back to him. His head moved and his eyes rolled. In my terror I expected him to get up and grapple me again. I quickly placed the muzzle of the pistol in his mouth and pulled the trigger." It was 5:30 a.m.

Stella made an official statement at city hall and also spoke with reporters soon after the shooting. She claimed that her endurance of the "drunken, unfaithful, vile" Smith ended "when he threatened to ruin my daughter." An autopsy indicated that the first shot had entered Smith's brain and probably killed him instantly. Stella was quickly taken into police custody and charged with first-degree murder. One report noted that she was held in the same cell that had been occupied by Gertrude Patterson, Helen Schmidlap and other notorious women charged with the same crime.

The trial began on March 12, 1917. Jurors were questioned about their views on the death penalty, but an acquittal, or at best a verdict of voluntary manslaughter, was all that was expected. The prosecution argued that

Stella Smith had premeditated the murder. Witnesses placed her outside, practicing shooting the gun before her estranged husband's arrival. They also cited her return to shoot him a second time—and to shoot him with the gun in his mouth—as evidence of premeditation. Moreover, one of the servants claimed that Stella had telephoned Smith and asked him to come over that night, while Stella maintained that Smith had somehow gained entry without permission.

The judge ordered the courtroom cleared of spectators during Stella's testimony. Stella testified with "fainting and nervousness" under direct examination and "cool determination" and anger under cross-examination. She listed many other incidents of Smith's degenerate and cruel behavior. Questioned repeatedly about her reasons for returning to the abusive Smith time and again, she proffered several explanations: "I was afraid for my life," "I wanted to remain friends with him" and "he repented for what he had done." Defense witnesses testified to the couple's frequent arguments, which generally related to Smith's demands for money. In any event, defense counsel argued that she should be vindicated "on the ground that she had submitted to indignities which…'even the law does not see fit to define in direct terms.'"

Stella was, without great debate within the jury, found not guilty and released from police custody. The verdict was one of several that Detective Sam Howe tagged as "rotten" in his murder book. Upon delivering the verdict, the judge stated, "The court instructed you that a woman has the same right to protect her home, her honor, her life, her child, as a man. This is the law and it covers every question involved in this case."

Chapter 4
"The Unwritten Law"

The "unwritten law defense" was recognized by nineteenth-century American juries. It acknowledged the right of a husband, father or brother to justifiably kill the man who "wronged" his female relative by sexual intimacy. The concept was broadened to encompass the inevitable "heat of passion" that was likely to occur when the wronged man learned of the seduction of a spouse or sweetheart, even if the guilty parties were not caught in the act. In some instances, a woman's desire to end a relationship seemed to be sufficient provocation.

CHARLES STICKNEY

"Do not see him, for I am afraid you may be tempted to put an end to the little worm."

On May 31, 1881, Charles W. Stickney, age thirty-seven, killed real estate agent Montgomery T. Campau, age unknown, and a young bride, Mrs. O.H. Devereux, age unknown. Stickney was a Harvard-educated teacher from the East Coast who had recently arrived in Denver with his (second) wife, Nina Stickney, and their young daughter. Stickney had difficulty securing employment in Denver and turned to prospecting in Gunnison to support his family. While he was gone, Nina became acquainted with Campau when she was searching for accommodations. According to one report, "Their acquaintance progressed so rapidly that one day in August Campau proposed a carriage ride. Mrs. Stickney consented…what followed the carriage ride may be known by the story told afterward in the court by Stickney."

Charles Stickney's entry in Detective Sam Howe's "murder book." *Sam Howe Collection, Colorado Historical Society.*

Later reports varied as to the nature of the relationship between Campau and Nina, with some stating that she was the initiator of their intimacy and others stating that he was. According to accounts given by both Stickney and his wife, Campau forcefully seduced Nina during the aforementioned carriage ride. Stickney approached Campau and demanded $10,000 in restitution for his "wounded honor" and to keep the matter quiet in the local press; it should be noted that some reports state that the money was demanded in order to provide for Nina, as he would soon be seeking a divorce. Campau acquiesced to his demands, offering him a $3,000 land deed and seven $1,000 promissory notes to be paid over time. At the time of the arrangement, overseen by Campau's lawyer, Stickney stated that he was no longer living with his wife.

However, after the deal was arranged, Stickney and Nina left Denver for Illinois. It was not long before Campau decided that he was dissatisfied with this arrangement and ceased paying restitution, claiming that the Stickneys were only attempting to blackmail him. The Stickneys returned to Denver to resolve the matter in court, but the legal expenses weighed heavily on

Stickney, and as one paper noted, "He became irritable and morbid." Matters worsened when he returned home to find Nina gone and a note explaining her departure: "You will not be able to succeed in your profession while you are hampered by this disgrace." She also warned him "not to shoot that little puppy—who is too small and mean and cowardly to own up. He must need to throw the blame on me. Do not see him, for I am afraid you may be tempted to put an end to the little worm."

These pleas were ineffectual, however, and on the evening of May 31, Stickney went to the boardinghouse at 420 Stout Street, where Campau lived. He entered the parlor and fired four shots, two of which struck Campau and one of which fatally struck innocent bystander Mrs. Devereux, who was staying at the boardinghouse with her husband and was unable to escape the scene quickly enough.

The trial began on February 7, 1882. Stickney pleaded not guilty to the murders by reason of insanity. According to one report, "Witnesses were brought from the far East to prove his character, and the insanity of some of his near relatives." Classmates from Harvard started a fund to cover the expenses of the trial. Stickney added drama to the proceedings, at one point leaping from his chair and yelling, "You're a liar!" when the prosecutor suggested that he had known of the intimacy between Campau and Nina before he returned from Gunnison. He had to be restrained, and "his mouth was frothing during this dramatic scene." It may have helped his case. Ultimately, the jury declared that Stickney was not guilty by reason of insanity.

The Stickney case is not a perfect exemplar of an "unwritten law" case, but there seems to be little doubt that the Campau-Nina sexual relationship weighed in Charles's favor. The theory of the defense, according to the *New York Times*, "was that Campau had betrayed Mrs. Stickney by force, and that the husband, acting under an uncontrollable impulse, had killed the destroyer of his honor."

CHARLES HENRY

"Captured by a siren."

Charles E. Henry, age nineteen, murdered Effie Moore, age nineteen, a song and dance actress, on November 14, 1887. Effie was performing as a "serio comic" at the Palace Theater on Fifteenth and Blake Streets, and this is where the homicide took place, in dramatic fashion.

Effie was from Kansas City. She had been married to variety actor Will Carroll for more than a year at the time of her death. Henry claimed that she had promised to marry him, and he had just discovered her relationship with Carroll. When she came off stage, he met her and went into a theater box with her. He confronted her about the marriage. He fired four shots at Effie, two of which were fatal.

Henry received the benefit of some sympathetic coverage. The *Rocky Mountain News* averred that "the woman was beautiful, and lured the boy into the theater where, under the pretense of love, she managed to bleed him of his money. He became insanely jealous because she was seen in company with a stranger, and entering a private box he shot her down in her tracks." Effie had to suffer additional indignities. The day after the shooting, her body was at the coroner's office awaiting the inquest. Members of the public were allowed to view the body in the reception room: "A young man stands at the head of the corpse, and as visitors approach raises the cloth that covers the body, showing the face and breast where the bullets entered."

Henry had only been in Denver for two weeks. He had been wildly spending his money—allegedly

Charles Henry. *Colorado State Archives.*

The shooting of Effie Moore by Charles Henry, as depicted by the *National Police Gazette.*

$4,000 or $5,000 in lottery winnings—during that time, apparently wanting to establish himself as a professional gambler. He now engaged the redoubtable defense lawyer Edgar Caypless. Henry's trial began on February 24, 1888. Although admittedly the shooter, he was portrayed as an innocent boy "captured by a siren." According to Caypless's closing argument, Henry "was the victim of this girl"; further, Henry "visited the gaming table, but it was to seek excitement" (rather, one presumes, than out of moral turpitude). The strategy worked. On February 26, Henry was acquitted.

This was not the end of the story. Henry left Denver for Texas. In 1892, he was arrested for the murder of Irene Russell, "an abandoned woman," in Dallas, Texas. On April 6 of that year, Russell was found on the banks of the Trinity River, with a revolver nearby, having been shot in the heart. The immediate verdict was suicide, but police learned that Henry had borrowed a gun on the night of Russell's death; it was the same gun found by the body. The similarities with the Moore case were obvious. The *News* picked up the story and noted that "another woman who could not marry him was ruthlessly shot down." The cases, indeed, were almost identical. On June 18, 1892, Henry was found not guilty of Russell's murder.

THE RYAN CASE

"Allow me to thank you very much for your kindness, and to assure you that it shall be the dying object of my life to repay it."

This case deals with the January 23, 1890 murder of Nellie Ryan, age twenty-two, who was murdered on her way to work at the Clinton Lunch Rooms at 1622 Curtis Street, where she was a waitress and cook, by Robert L. Scott (real surname Vernon), age between twenty-eight and thirty, a cook in a Champa Street restaurant. At the time of the murder, which took place at 6:00 a.m., Nellie had been walking to work with her sister, Agnes, and a friend, Annie Keough. They reached the corner of Champa and Fourteenth before a man stepped out from under a tree and ran up to Nellie. He tapped her on the shoulder; when she turned, he put a gun to her side and shot her. The bullet, however, hit one of her steel corset stays and did not injure her. A second shot was immediately fired as Nellie opened her mouth to scream; this one was effective. She died on the street a few minutes later. The attacker fled but was soon identified as R.L. Scott. Scott had been hounding Nellie since March of the previous year.

The precipitating incident for the stalking occurred when both Nellie and Scott worked at the Clinton restaurant. Scott made an indecent proposal to Nellie. She rebuked him and told him that she would make a report to the proprietor if he repeated it. Scott persisted and Nellie made her report; Scott was fired. He began to follow Nellie constantly and called at her residence on Thirteenth Street. Nellie reportedly struck him with a horsewhip to get him to leave. On August 5, he located Nellie near her home and assaulted her (the nature of the assault was unspecified). Her screams drove him away, and Nellie was determined to have him arrested. He was tried and fined in the justice court.

A few days later, Nellie received a letter that read: "Denver, Colo., Aug., 1889—Miss Nellie Ryan: Allow me to thank you very much for your kindness, and to assure you that it shall be the dying object of my life to repay it. A man does not forget many things, but he would not be human could he forget the deed you did to me. It may be for days and it may be for years, but certainly I will repay you with interest some day.—R.L.S."

Nellie was terrified, but her friends persuaded her that the letter was a bluff. Then she heard that Scott had moved to Colorado Springs and felt assured that the problem was over. However, she had no idea that Scott had returned to Denver two weeks before the shooting and had taken the Champa restaurant job. He was drinking heavily and became angry when he learned that Nellie had moved. He was able to get her new address from the White Cooks and Waiters' Society and planned his encounter with her on January 3.

The problem was apprehending Scott after he ran from the scene; he had a twenty-five-minute lead before police took up the search. Various alleged sightings of Scott were investigated, and his description was circulated. The *Rocky Mountain News* noted that "Scott's personal appearance would cause a man to distrust him," though his most notable characteristic seemed to be his walk ("in walking he swings his shoulders instead of his hands, and for that reason can be recognized [at] a long distance"). Aside from Scott, police investigated other suspects, including W.G. Barnes, who was said to be an admirer of Agnes Ryan's. James Atkins, who was arrested near Fort Logan, bore a resemblance to Scott and had recently purchased a revolver. However, these suspects were not Scott.

On February 8, the body of a suicide victim at Pueblo was identified as Scott. He was found dead of a gunshot to the head near the San Carlos station on the Denver and Rio Grande Railroad. No one seemed entirely positive of the identification, and Scott's acquaintances differed widely on the resemblance of the body to the Scott they knew. An editorial in the

Nellie Ryan (left) and the body of the man identified as Robert L. Scott (right). The strap around the neck was necessary to keep the body in place, as "the effect of decomposition [was] very marked."

Central City Weekly Register-Call pointed out that Scott might have aged since his official departure from Denver and especially during his time as a fugitive. This argument did not seem to convince the doubters. Scott, who was born in Scotland, had allegedly received a money inheritance, and it was suggested that he may have returned to that country.

C. Burdette Bell

"I believe that any man fit to be called a man would do exactly as I did under the circumstances."

The December 28, 1908 murder of Cuthbert Cuvier Dury (aka J. Byron Allenton), age twenty-nine, an actor and the son of ornithologist Charles Dury, by laundry wagon driver C. Burdette Bell, age twenty-five, is another case in point.

Burdette and his wife, Mabel Bell, age twenty, had moved to Denver three years before the incident; they had one small child. Mabel, an aspiring actress, left Bell for Dury after becoming acquainted with him through his advertisement seeking young women for stage productions. Dury had also abandoned his own wife, a consumptive who was living with her mother "in a tent in Englewood." At the time of the murder, Mabel and Dury were living together at the Leon apartments at 1523 Curtis Street. The murder occurred in the hallway of the Leon apartments. "Dury pushed me against the wall and choked me," Bell testified. "The thought came to me that he would do me bodily injury and perhaps kill me and run away

Mabel Bell (left)
and C. Cuvier Dury
(right).

with my wife and little baby. I wanted to get out into the hall and talk it over with him." Bell fired five shots at Dury (four finding their target) and then escaped from the building. He surrendered himself to the police half an hour later.

Mabel's testimony was markedly different, stating that Bell had arrived at the apartment asking to speak with her. By her account, "Dury suggested that she put on her coat to cover the kimona she was wearing and the two went into the hall to see Bell. As they passed through the door, according to Mrs. Bell, her husband grasped her arm, saying: 'Oh, you are undressed, are you?' He then pushed her back through the door. Almost immediately firing was heard in the hallway." Mabel escaped through a window, climbed the fire escape to the floor above and hid in a room, where she was soon discovered by the police.

Bell was expected to plead the "unwritten law" but instead pleaded self-defense, stating that he would avoid "brain storms, emotional insanity or anything else of that kind" during the trial and that he should bc admired for his honesty and convictions. However, his statements follow a well-established pattern that has nothing to do with self-defense: "I will trust my case to the hands of any twelve men that you can pick up in the streets. I believe that any man fit to be called a man would do exactly as I did under the circumstances. Another man stole my wife. I killed him. Now, what is there wrong in that?"

During the trial, Mabel stated that Bell had not supported her for several months and that she had been working at different things to help support herself and her child. Moreover, she averred that she had decided to break up with Dury and had told him so. She allegedly requested a visit with

Burdette Bell in prison. *Colorado State Archives.*

her husband while he was incarcerated during the trial: "I think now that everything is clear. Bert was right and Dury and I all wrong. I want to see Bert and tell him so." Her request, however, was refused.

On February 11, 1909, Bell was found guilty of voluntary manslaughter and was sentenced to serve five to eight years at Canon City. Bell, as a final request, asked Judge H.L. Shattuck to make arrangements for his twenty-one-month-old daughter, as he believed that Mabel was an unfit mother. This request was granted, and the baby was sent to the nursery of the House of the Good Shepherd. A report in the *Aspen Democrat* noted that "with absolutely no manifestation of sympathy, Mrs. Mabel Perkins Bell bade her husband goodby [*sic*] at the Union depot yesterday morning as Bell left for Canon City to begin his sentence of from five to eight years for the murder of C. Cuvior Dury. A few hours later Mrs. Bell was laughing and chatting merrily with a male companion at Sixteenth and Curtis streets."

Mabel later obtained a divorce from Bell during his incarceration. She remarried (to Charles Porter), but in April 1915, she divorced him as well.

HENRY ROBITAILLE

"Of course I'm sorry, but then she's as well off where she is as she was working down there in the restaurant with those Japs."

The August 7, 1912 murder of Pearl Robitaille (née Caldwell or Cadwell), age twenty-four, by her teamster husband Henry, age twenty-five, unexpectedly sheds a light on Denver's Japanese community. Pearl worked at a Japanese restaurant located at 1917 Larimer Street, and that is where the murder took place.

Henry Robitaille went to the restaurant and demanded five dollars from Pearl. (Robitaille's surname caused no end of confusion to his contemporaries; it is often rendered as Robitelli or some variation thereof, and he is misidentified as Italian in some sources.) When she refused, he shot her twice in the back and then began shooting at the employees and patrons of the restaurant. His other shots went wild. He left the restaurant, and three hours later, he turned up at the Argo Saloon twenty

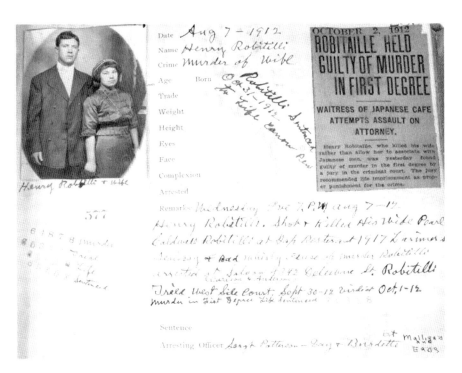

Henry and Pearl Robitaille in Detective Sam Howe's "murder book." *Sam Howe Collection, Colorado Historical Society.*

blocks away. He demanded all the cash in the drawer but did not take it; instead, he forced the bartender to serve him whiskey. When he relaxed, he was overpowered and taken to the city jail. There he fell unconscious. Out of fear that he had ingested poison, he was rushed to the county hospital. His condition was later diagnosed as acute alcoholism. Pearl died within a few minutes of the shooting.

Henry asserted, "I was drunk when I shot her. Of course I'm sorry, but then she's as well off where she is as she was working down there in the restaurant with those Japs." He claimed that he had no intention of shooting Pearl when he entered the restaurant. However, authorities believed that he planned the crime. Witnesses stated that Henry, when leaving work that day, had shown them his revolver and said that he intended to kill his wife. Pearl had left him a month earlier and had been avoiding him since that time. She refused to tell him where she was living and refused to return to him. The Japanese proprietor of the restaurant had unwittingly exposed Pearl to danger. When Henry came in, the man told Pearl to speak to Henry and persuade him to go away.

Henry Robitaille in prison. *Colorado State Archives.*

On August 9, the *Post* announced that "white girls will be barred from Jap restaurants" in response to the homicide. Specifically, they would be barred from employment in those establishments by police patrols. The article noted that "Robitaille asserts his crime was due to the belief that his wife had cast him off for a Japanese and he considered she would be better off dead than associating with the Orientals."

Henry Robitaille was found guilty of first-degree murder on October 1. He was sentenced to life in prison. His sentence was later commuted to twenty-five years, and reports stated that he hoped that even that would be halved; in fact, he was paroled in January 1924.

Chapter 5

Unsolved

D enver has its share of unsolved cases that still intrigue historians. These cases also reveal a great deal about the investigative practices of the period, as police detectives examined and reexamined evidence, located suspects and posited various theories to explain the crimes.

THE DENVER STRANGLER

"The chief of police could rid this city of its company of male vampires, known as the macquereaux."

The well-known "Denver Strangler" case of 1894 falls into this category. It has been discussed at length elsewhere, but it is worth a quick summary here. The Strangler is generally accepted to have claimed three victims: German-born Lena Tapper, age thirty-seven, on September 3 at 1911 Market Street; French-born Marie Contassoit (aka Contassot), age twenty-three, on October 28 at 1925 Market Street; and Japanese-born Kiku Oyama, age twenty-four, on November 13 at 1957 Market Street. The women, all prostitutes, were found strangled in their rooms. The *News* noted that all three had left their rear doors unlocked, which meant access from the back alley was easy. Two later cases that are usually linked with the Strangler, the deaths of Julia Voght and Mabel Brown, occurred in 1898 and 1903, respectively.

Robbery did not appear to be a motive in the three original cases, so the personal relationships of the women became the investigative focus.

Left to right: victim Lena Tapper; the Market Street residences of the three victims; and victim Kiku Oyama. *Sam Howe Collection, Colorado Historical Society (image at left).*

The main suspect in the Denver Strangler case was Richard Demady, age forty-three. Demady was Tapper's lover and landlord. The best motive that could be ascribed to him was his relationship with another prostitute, Laura Johnson (aka Lilly Belmont), who had been the cause of quarrels between himself and Tapper. Still, as defense counsel asserted, Demady and Tapper were not married; he was free to leave her whenever he wished.

Demady was charged with first-degree murder in Tapper's death. His trial began on April 20, 1895, amid reports that he had attempted to bribe both judge and witnesses to obtain an acquittal. George Copeland, a white porter at Mattie Silks's bordello, and Sadie Crow, an African American woman, testified that they had seen Demady abusing and choking Tapper on the night of the crime. Their credibility was damaged by other witnesses; while Crow and Copeland claimed not to be acquainted, they had actually known each other for more than two years. Another witness called to testify to Demady's violent treatment of Tapper, one Belle Gross, changed her testimony on the stand. Now she had only seen a smiling Demady shake Tapper lightly. Demady was ultimately acquitted on May 11, 1895; thereafter, he was rumored to have relocated to Brazil. The trial reputedly cost the county $4,000 and thus was considered a "high-priced fiasco."

Other suspects in the case were Charles Challou (aka Challoup), Contassoit's pimp. He was arrested soon after her murder but never tried. Challou had made a considerable amount of money from Contassoit and her sister; however, she had recently left him for Tony Sanders (aka Antonio Sanpietro) and was demanding that Challou return her share of her earnings

Richard Demady in Detective Sam Howe's "murder book." *Sam Howe Collection, Colorado Historical Society.*

and jewelry. Sanders, a police messenger, seemed eager to put the blame on Challou and/or Demady, but the attempt backfired. Sanders himself was arrested on October 29, 1894, in connection with Contassoit's death. Alfonse LeMaire, a vagabond French sailor, was arrested on January 2, 1895, when Victor Monchereaux (aka Monchanaint) reported him to police for his alleged remarks about the murders (e.g., regarding Contassoit, "There is from $8,000 to $9,000 in that house, I believe, and I will kill her to get that money").

Additional suspects were Frank Roch, a "miserable, despised and very degraded saloon menial" who was seen running down the alley at time of Oyama's murder; H. Moller, an Italian who had been arrested for assaulting a woman; and Henri Gutig, who was sought in connection with threatening Nellie Hicks, another Denver prostitute. Nothing came of these investigations, and the case remained unsolved: "The Frenchmen are so banded together now that it seems impossible to get any of them to talk on any subject."

The Strangler case is closely tied in with the activities of the macquereaux, also known as "Les Chevaliers d'Amour" or the French underground. (Gutig was tagged with the appellation "king of the [Denver] macquereaux" during the investigation.) Macquereaux were, in fact, active in many major American cities other than Denver, including New York City, Chicago, Los Angeles and Salt Lake City; they primarily trafficked in prostitution and white slavery. Operating largely out of the red-light district on Market Street, the macquereaux were active in bringing prostitutes into Denver from foreign locations—France most often, though not exclusively. "The trial of Demady settled all doubt as to the existence of a society of macquereaux in Denver," the *Post* asserted. "There are several hundred Frenchwomen in Denver who are slaves." The same was reportedly true of the Japanese community. Promised well-paying jobs by procurers in their home countries, the women had a bitter surprise in America when they were trapped in brothels with few possibilities for escape.

According to a report in the *News*, citing Joseph Walker, head of the U.S. Secret Service in Denver, and Louis Adams, inspector for the U.S. Immigration Bureau, "The chief of police could rid this city of its company of male vampires, known as the macquereaux, within five days' time if they chose to do so…That the city government is responsible for the existence of this band of owners of white slaves was the emphatic opinion of the three government officials."

The issue arose periodically in the press. In 1906, for example, "Three men charged with importing girls into the United States for immoral purposes were discovered to be in Pueblo. They were accused of the violation of the immigration laws, found guilty by a federal grand jury in New York…and the men Anatole Harshaw, Frank Naubert, and Henry Noll, were sent to prison." However, these cases were not isolated events. The *News* noted that the prosecution of these cases was difficult, given that many of the men involved were U.S. citizens and accomplished their purposes by coordinating with a variety of individuals abroad.

In Denver itself, efforts to deal with the problem of the macquereaux and white slavery included regular sweeps of Market Street to attempt to purge the brothels of undocumented workers by asking for their documentation, comparing it to official records and questioning them. However, this tended to be ineffectual as a technique, as the women would simply deny accusations that they were the individuals documented in government registers.

One case associated with the Strangler murders was the October 7, 1898 death of Julia Voght (aka Nannie Voght or Wright), a clairvoyant and medium. Voght, age forty, was well known in Denver not only because of her profession but also because of her dramatic appearance—she had

Julia and Julius Voght.

red hair and wore clothing "usually affected by a girl of sixteen." She was married to Julius Voght, who had been charged with grand larceny for theft of public goods, receiving stolen goods and stealing seven bicycles. At the time of her murder, he was serving a sentence of nine years at the state penitentiary.

Julia was found dead in her apartment at 2020 Champa Street. She had been strangled, and her death was immediately linked to the killer of Tapper, Contassoit and Oyama. She was also said to be the psychic who approached police in 1894 claiming to know the identity of the Strangler. Thus, it was suggested that the murderer had killed her because she knew of his involvement with the murders in 1894; perhaps he "was also a believer in 'spirits' and decided to put her out of the way and possibly save himself from exposure." (In fact, after Voght's murder, another psychic, Mrs. D.J. Moran, came forward and claimed to have predicted Voght's death: "I told Nannie she was going to be killed and warned her to be careful." One wonders if someone predicted Mrs. Moran's death and if the Cassandra-like chain of psychics remained unbroken.)

George Randell (aka Randall), age unknown, an African American man, was arrested the next day (October 8, 1898) for Voght's murder. Julius Voght wrote a letter to the police from prison, stating that he believed Randell was his wife's killer based on his long history of borrowing money from Julia. Other sources implied that Randell had been involved in running various scams with Julia, and the two previously had a violent disagreement over their business. There was no solid evidence linking him to the murder, however, and he was soon released from custody. Detective Loomis noted that "every circumstance pointed to Randall's innocence…Granting that he had committed [the crime], he would never have returned to the house the next morning. A negro is superstitious and always looks with the greatest horror on a dead body. Afterward, when the detectives took Randall and forced him to view the corpse, he could never have withstood the ordeal had he murdered the woman." Randell was undoubtedly pleased to be exonerated, for whatever reason.

The Denver Strangler was also mentioned in connection with the death of prostitute Mabel Brown (aka Maude) in the early morning hours of July 6, 1903. Brown, age twenty, lived at 1931 Market Street. She had allegedly been engaged to Henry T. "Harry" Challis, age thirty, a bartender at Bob Warner's Saloon. The cause of Brown's death was first reported as strangulation. Water was also found in her lungs; however, the physicians who conducted the autopsy believed that strangulation was the primary cause of death. Suspects in the case included her ex-lover, Samuel Holzweig, whom she had thrown over for Challis, as well as, of course, Challis himself, who had postponed the wedding despite her wishes to marry and quit working

Exterior and interior of Mabel Brown's residence at 1931 Market Street.

as a prostitute. The Denver police did not suspect the French macquereaux in this case, an assessment based on the testimonies of the other women of the district.

Challis was taken into custody immediately, and police reports indicated that there was a great deal of evidence against him. He was charged with Brown's murder on July 15. The judge, however, ended up dismissing the case and releasing Challis from police custody on July 21. This news incited concern among the women of Market Street, given the history of violence against women in the area, but any connection with the Strangler cases appeared unlikely.

Russell Boles

"I heard him swear at me and that was the last thing I knew."

On December 31, 1901, Florence Fridborn, age sixteen, was raped, and her brother Harold, age fourteen, was murdered. The Fridborn home was located at 2734 Gray Street, about two blocks from a small lake located at Lake Avenue and Alcott Street. At about 8:30 p.m., Florence and Harold went out to skate. While they were putting on their skates, they saw a man approaching the lake. Florence was suspicious of him, but Harold said, "The man only wants to see us skate." When the man came down the bank, he asked them if the skating was any good; the Fridborns replied in the negative, since there were several holes in the ice. The man then drew an axe from behind him and asked if they had any money. They said no, but he insisted on searching them and ordered them not to make a sound, saying that he would not hurt them if they did as he said.

He made them lie down on the bank. Harold offered him the contents of his pockets—a knife and a few peanuts—but the man was not interested. According to Florence, "After he made us lay down on the bank, he sat on me. My brother coaxed him to let me up. The man told him to shut up. He would not do it, so the man hit him with the axe." Harold groaned, and the man struck him again and then began choking Florence. She struggled and kicked, and the man put his hand over her mouth; she bit his fingers. Then "I heard him swear at me and that was the last thing I knew" until she regained consciousness. She was alone and assumed Harold had gone for help. Florence staggered home. She

Florence Fridborn (left) and Harold Fridborn.

had lost her cape and cap, her clothing was torn and muddy and she had a black eye, marks on her throat and badly bloodshot eyes. A doctor's examination confirmed that she had been sexually assaulted.

Florence provided a detailed description of her assailant: bearded, about thirty-six years old, medium height, with calloused hands and wearing a dark-colored overcoat and a plain gold band on one finger. One detail that would prove controversial later was her description of the attacker's speech: "His voice was gruff but medium; I noticed an accent in his voice, and his color was the reason I thought him a foreigner."

According to the *News*, police "were kept at work rounding up suspicious characters in different parts of the city." Moreover, by the next day "the scene of the murder at the foot of an embankment surrounding a small pond of water at the intersection of Lake Avenue, Alcott Street and Fife Court, was visited by at least 1,000 people yesterday…who picked up pieces of sticks and stones to take away as souvenirs of the crime." This certainly did not make their job easier. It is difficult to follow the early stages of the investigation in the press, which reported several near-identifications by Florence; these may have been false reports, since court records note that she remained consistent in naming one suspect, and one only, as the attacker.

Russell Boles (aka Bolles), age thirty-three and a musician, soon became the prime suspect. Boles had a wife and two sons in Otero, but his excessive drinking was the likely cause of the failed marriage. His case provides a rare glimpse of the lives of Denver street people during the era; his activities immediately before and after the time of the murder were covered in detail in the trial transcript.

Boles appears to have spent December 31 aimlessly. He went to the home of J.A. Cox at Thirty-second and Bert Street, where he sometimes stayed; he found Cox in the process of bundling up some celery that he wanted

The impromptu skating pond at intersection of Lake Avenue, Alcott Street and Fife Court, where the crime occurred (best image available).

to sell that day. Boles agreed to take out Cox's wagon and do the selling. A cigar maker named Charles Fitzmyer was also present and was able to testify to Boles's dark overcoat and facial hair. He was also present when Boles returned "late in the night" with three bloody fingers.

Boles left some of the proceeds of the celery sale, but not all, at Cox's house. He then went to Tony Volo's saloon at the corner of Thirty-seventh and Bell, arriving there between 10:00 and 11:00 p.m. He encountered Tommy Olford, Mike (or John) Coombs and Bert Jones—referred to collectively by witnesses as "the boys"—and the group moved back and forth from that saloon to Herman Wassenich's, drinking continuously. They noticed that Boles was eager to wash his hands but did not notice whether he was injured. The boys "made him go back to Cox's" at about 2:00 a.m.

The next morning, they saw him at 11:00 a.m. in Tony Volo's saloon again. Boles was thrown out by the bartender after repeatedly falling asleep in the wine room. They noticed that "his finger was tied up." The bartender also told them that Boles had thrown away his underwear in the water closet and that "we was joshing him about it." Boles went to the house of Mary Stephenson at 1767 West Thirty-fourth and Witter, where he had rented a room in the past. Stephenson, who was very deaf and was questioned through an ear trumpet, said that *he was drinking a little and there was some boys that was teasing him and he asked me for a room, that he could lie down, and I was talking to him and those boys came up the stairs and came in…One of the boys says, "I will take him away," and they started, and he seemed to be unfortunate; Mr. Boles came back; those boys were knocking him down in the street and running over him and pounding him with their hats, and I says to my grand daughter, "If I had known this I would have given him a room."*

She did not notice anything wrong with Boles's fingers. The boys, predictably, took Boles back to the saloon. Later that day, after parting company, they saw Boles coming out of a barbershop, cleanshaven.

Finally, Dr. Franklin Dabney later testified that he dressed a man's fingers on January 1. Dabney thought that the wounds were consistent with bite marks, and the man fit Boles's description. The man claimed that he did not have the funds to pay the two-dollar doctor's fee. (It is worth noting that Dabney's testimony was controversial at trial; unlike the other witnesses, he did not come forward until Boles was brought back to Denver and appeared in court in 1903. Further, Dabney had not made a written record of the visit at the time it occurred.)

In any event, before he could be arrested, Boles left Denver on January 8. He later testified that he traveled through a number of cities—Colorado Springs, Pueblo, Trinidad, Gallup (New Mexico), Williams (Arizona), Los Angeles, San Francisco, Sacramento and Seattle—working as a laborer on jobs that lasted from two days to five weeks. He used the name "Bert Jewel" as an alias. Boles explained that he did not want his wife to know where he was, alluding to a custody dispute.

In the interim, Florence Fridborn faced another traumatic incident. The *Rocky Mountain News* published an article on July 24, 1902, falsely stating that she had just given birth to a child as the result of the rape. She sued for damages for libel in the amount of $10,000. The case was tried by jury, resulting in a verdict in Florence's favor; however, the *News* appealed, denying that it published the article maliciously, stating that the article was incorrect but based on reasonable authority and noting that a retraction was published the next day. In September 1909, the Colorado Supreme Court reversed the trial court's judgment, based on rather suspect reasoning (the *News* had an honest belief in the truth of the story, though it was based on a dubious information swap with a reporter from the *Republican*, and no attempt was made to verify it; moreover, though it was considered libelous to say that an unmarried woman was pregnant and thus unchaste, a rape victim was not libeled in the same circumstances because she had not acted unchastely).

On September 25, 1903, Boles was apprehended in Westminster, British Columbia. Mr. Fridborn and Florence were brought to Canada, courtesy of the *Denver Post*, to see the suspect. At the New Westminster jail, Florence positively identified Boles as her attacker. However, he was not placed in a lineup or viewed with other prisoners, and this procedural irregularity was a key issue in the case thereafter. Based on the identification, Boles was returned to Denver and charged with murder and rape on November 18.

Boles's trial began in February 1904. It was well attended, with many female spectators in attendance. Issues presented included the quality of the lighting near the pond (witnesses testified to their adequacy or inadequacy in terms of making out a face), the "foreigner" description by Florence, Boles's speech and gait, whether his cap would have obscured his face, whether Boles had ever worn a gold ring and whether he had been bearded, cleanshaven or something in between on the night of the crime.

The prosecutor attempted to paint a picture of Boles's poor relationships with women, asking questions like, "You were forced to marry your wife, weren't you?" and, "Were you arrested in Sullivan, Indiana…for 'monkeying' with some girls?" Defense counsel tried to argue that a "paramour" of Florence's might have been the guilty party, since her skates were found at the pond strapped together and her cape was folded. He repeatedly suggested that the *Denver Post* had a vendetta against Boles, emphasized the "tainted" nature of the single-person viewing of Boles in New Westminster and presented a partial alibi: a Mrs. Cross, from Boles's home state of Indiana, recalled that he had visited her home on the evening of December 31. Much discussion of whether Mrs. Cross had later written a letter saying that she was mistaken about the date of Boles's visit ensued, as well as whether the "Indiana delegation" was to be believed.

Boles then took the stand. He refused to answer some questions but claimed at trial that he had injured his finger while working at the Denver Box Company *before* Christmas and had worn a bandage for a day or two.

On March 6, 1904, Boles was found guilty of first-degree murder and sentenced to life in prison. He appealed the judgment, but the Colorado Supreme Court affirmed the lower court in 1906. This happened in spite of the opinion of the *Times* that "it is an open secret among police officers and detectives that none of them believe Russell Boles guilty of the killing of Harold Fridborn." Since the case against Boles was viewed as the *Denver Post*'s baby, the comment may have been due to competitiveness rather

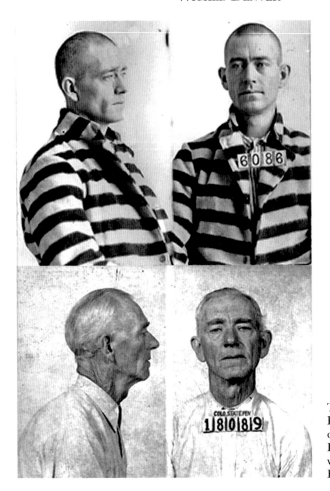

Two mug shots of Russell Boles: when convicted in the Fridborn case (top) and when convicted for the Boulder offense (bottom).

than fact. However, rather surprisingly, the State Board of Pardons decided that Boles was, in fact, innocent, and he was unconditionally pardoned by Governor George A. Carlson and released from the penitentiary on January 12, 1916.

Some details of Boles's life after prison are available. By 1920, he was back in Sullivan, Indiana, living with his sister. He later moved to Longmont, where in 1933 he reappeared in the press as "Russell Boles, 63, victim of a tragic miscarriage of justice." He requested compensation from the state for his twelve years in prison, arguing that he had lost his best earning years and needed income in his old age. (Of course, it is unlikely that Boles would have spent those twelve years productively, if his pre-prison behavior means anything.) The outcome of the suit is unknown; technically, the Fridborn case is unsolved. What is known is that Boles returned to the penitentiary at Canon City later in life; he was found guilty of another sexual assault, this one in Boulder County. He died in 1941.

The Capitol Hill Slugger

"The world would be better off if there were no women."

Echoes of the Strangler abounded in the case of the "Capitol Hill Slugger." In 1900 and 1901, a series of assaults on Denver women led to three deaths, a trial and an inconclusive end. While not quite rising to the level of "epidemic hysteria" or "collective delusion"—terms used to describe a community-wide suggestibility and panic—the sheer number of cases attributed to the Slugger is surprising. A partial list:

- Celestine Coleman, age seventeen, June 24, 1900, at 3022 Alcott Street, Highlands
- Mrs. Alva Jessup, age unknown, August 24, 1900, in front of Temple Emmanuel
- Sophia Salomon, age unknown, August 24, 1900, near her home at 1738 Pearl Street
- Sadie McDonald, age unknown, August 24, 1900, at Twelfth and Washington Avenue
- Lillian Bell, age about forty-five, August 24, 1900, at Sixteenth and Washington
- Annie McAtee, age thirty-eight, October 5, 1900, in the alley of Thirty-first and Humboldt
- Emma Carlson, age twenty-three, October 11, 1900, at Tenth Avenue and Emerson
- Hattie Stoepel, age seventeen, October 13, 1900, at 1051 South Fifteenth Street
- Marion Hard, age unknown, October 16, 1900
- Maud Dunseath, age twenty, October 16, 1900
- Mrs. Dewert E. Young, age unknown, in front of the Corona school
- Julia Dohr, age forty-eight, January 6, 1902, on Sixteenth Avenue and Ogden Street
- Marie Frazer, age nineteen, February 16, 1901, on Twenty-ninth and Humboldt Street

- Mary Short, age forty, February 22, 1901, between Colfax and Sixteenth
- Emma Johnson, age thirty, February 22, 1901, at 1924 Pennsylvania Avenue
- Josephine Unternahrer, age thirty-six, February 22, 1901, between Pennsylvania Avenue and Pearl Street near Nineteenth Avenue
- Mary Eisenhart, age fourteen, April 18, 1901, at Twenty-eighth and Lawrence Street
- Eliza "Lizzie" Monroe, age fifty, April 20, 1901, at Downing and Twenty-fifth Avenue

With the exception of Lillian Bell, Josephine Unternahrer, and Mary Short, the women survived the attacks. The Slugger's *modus operandi* was to approach lone women on the street and strike them on the head with some object that often cracked their skulls (according to newspapers, possibly a sap, the butt of a gun, a sandbag or a combination of weapons). The attacker thus acquired the titles of the "Capitol Hill Slugger," the "Capitol Hill Thug" and the "Sandbagger." His motives were unclear, particularly in light of the fact that only some of the victims were robbed. The attacks generated a wave of public interest and alarm, as well as speculation: "Veteran detectives and police officials all declare that crime has rapidly increased since the abolishment of capital punishment two years ago."

Albert Cowan, age forty-two, was picked up by police as a "suspicious character" on February 25, 1901. Like many of the other "usual suspects" in these cases, he drew police attention by his extreme statements and unusual behavior. However, reports suggest that there was no evidence against him

Four victims of the Slugger. *Left to right*: Emma Johnson, Josephine Unternahrer, Mary Short and Lillian Bell.

at the time of the arrest, though he was quickly identified by one of the victims, Mary Short, who later died. When questioned at the jail, he appeared to be "mentally unbalanced," claiming to have been persecuted by women. When asked by Police Captain Armstrong why he had been persecuted, he replied, "I was. I hate them, but I'll not tell you anymore; I don't trust anyone." He was formally charged on February 27.

Before the trial, a letter was received by the Denver police from Raton, New Mexico. It stated that Cowan had been known in Las Vegas as "Bug House Davis," an ice peddler at the hot springs. The writer of the letter, W.H. Howe, stated that Davis raved "like a mad man, saying the world would be better off if there were no women…and said that in a few years the women would all be killed off."

Cowan's trial in the death of Mary Short began on March 30, 1901. Among those who testified was Albert Frederick, who stated that he

Albert Cowan, the prime suspect.

"was crossing a vacant lot when he saw a woman pass him. He heard her cry out when she was past him and looking around, he saw a man standing over her with his arm upraised and something shining in his hand." However, he also stated that "he hastened on as he did not want to be mixed up in any fight." Shortly thereafter, he was passed by a man whom he identified in the courtroom as Cowan.

The cross-examination of Frederick is worth mentioning, as the defense questioned his credibility on the basis of his race; although Frederick was of Arabian descent, the attorney insisted that because Frederick had lived in "colored barracks" while he was in the army and had worked at a "colored barbershop," he was thus "colored" too. This line of questioning eventually angered Frederick, who "fairly raved over it and finally caught up a revolver and said that Reese [the attorney] was a dirty skunk and that he would kill him." The attorney also made the argument that Frederick himself was responsible for the attacks, although no charges were officially levied at that time (later, charges against Frederick would be filed, although he was not found guilty). Ultimately, Frederick's testimony was discredited by the arguments of the attorney, as well as two other witnesses who stated that Frederick had been in the barracks that night and could not have seen the attack take place.

Other witnesses, however, offered damaging testimony, including that of a young man named W.G. Hansen, who identified Cowan as a customer at his hardware store. Cowan had recently purchased "two hammer handles, the heaviest they had." Another witness, Bartholomew Julien, a car inspector for the Union Pacific, identified Cowan as the man he saw running past his house moments after Annie McAtee was assaulted. However, Cowan also produced an eleventh-hour alibi for February 22: his landlord at the Bristol House Hotel at Nineteenth and Larimer testified that Cowan was in the hotel from 6:30 until after 9:00 p.m., when he went out to pick up some baggage from the Phoenix House. He returned to the Bristol and did not leave his room thereafter. All of his time was accounted for by the landlords of the two hotels, with the exception of fifteen minutes—too short a time to commit the assaults of that night.

Cowan was, in the end, discharged on April 11, 1901, for lack of evidence but was "immediately rearrested on charge of insanity," the jury being concerned that he was a danger to himself and others. He was released again shortly and told reporters that he intended to go to Central City to seek work, since he had become notorious in Denver. The *Aspen Tribune* noted that "he said with every expression of disgust that some woman out in California had written to him for his photograph." It is worth noting that slugging cases involving robbery were a regular occurrence in the 1890s—a fact that seemingly was forgotten—and men were victims in slugging cases as well over the two decades, though none of them was tagged as a Slugger victim.

THE STRANGE DEATH OF SIGNE CARLZEN

"Her life was good, but her death will do more good."

Signe Amelia Carlzen (aka Signa, Carlsen or Carlson), age thirty-two, was a music teacher in the Montclair area of Denver. She lived with her parents at 1908 Quebec Street. By all accounts, she was serious, dedicated to her work (she had more than thirty students) and sensible; as a friend noted, "she gave no time to small vanities." She sang, played both the piano and the cornet and occasionally took professional performance engagements.

On August 11, 1912, Carlzen visited the home of William W. Goodsell at Leetsdale and South Holly Streets for a scheduled piano lesson with Goodsell's two daughters. The lesson went off as planned, and Carlzen departed just before 8:00 p.m. on the mile-and-a-half walk to the Fourth Avenue streetcar line. At some point in her journey on a lonely road between Montclair and Aurora—one source identifies the location as being near East Alameda Avenue and South Forest (sometimes Fir) Street—she was savagely attacked with an axe.

Signe Carlzen.

The physically fit and athletic Carlzen put up a vigorous fight, apparently gouging the perpetrator with a hatpin, the broken stub of which was still clutched in her hand. She received several mortal blows to the head. Police were of the opinion that she was sexually assaulted after death and that "the lower part of her body was mutilated with a knife." Her broken watch, found about one hundred feet farther up the road, set the time of the attack at about 8:15 p.m. One of her stockings had been stuffed in her mouth. Her body was discovered at about 9:00 a.m. the next day by dairyman D.A. Talcott, who was out rounding up his cows. Other evidence recovered from the scene included a broken pair of eyeglasses, scattered sheet music and a bloodstained handkerchief. A bloody fingerprint was visible on the watch. No axe or other weapon was found.

Signe's parents had a relationship that is almost the stuff of comedy. They had fallen out in 1891, divorced and continued to live on the same property thereafter without speaking to each other. Signe sided with her mother, and they occupied the main house, along with her two brothers. Sven M. Carlzen, her father, lived in a shanty nearby.

There were suggestions that Sven may have been the attacker. A devotee of palmistry, he quickly claimed to have predicted an early death for Signe: "I knew my daughter would meet a violent death. The reading of her hand told me the tale years ago. She had an island on her life line, as it was held up to me, and I knew what that meant." The *Post* noted that "the father was at times morose and possessed of a quick temper. Neighbors say that rumor is that their separation was caused by the cruelty of the father to both mother and children." Signe's student Mildred Goodsell recalled that "on one occasion she remarked that her father was dead to her. I did not ask her what she meant by that." Sven himself had a peculiar reaction to Signe's death: "Her life was good, but her death will do more good…It was her duty to go, and she went."

Police wondered if a spurned admirer could have been involved, but Signe's parents said that she "had no men friends, and lived for her mother and her work." Police hypothesized that she was attacked at the location where the watch was found and dragged toward the only building in the area, an abandoned dwelling known as the Burns House. Reputedly haunted, it may have served as a convenient vantage point for the perpetrator to lie in wait. Carlzen had mentioned that she believed she had been followed on the previous few nights but did not seem concerned.

The truly odd aspect of the Carlzen case was the bizarre array of suspects—no two resembled each other. At about 6:00 p.m. on the evening of the crime, a dairyman's daughter named Olga Kaiser (aka Keiser), age eleven, met a man near the old Burns House. He was about thirty years old, wore a light gray suit with a light straw hat and had a sallow, thin face, dark eyes and a powerful form. He said, "I want to talk to you. What block is this?" Olga was on horseback, but his manner frightened her. She said that she didn't know and "galloped away on the horse and watched him at a safe distance. He looked so mad that I guess he wanted to kill me." The man walked away toward the Burns House.

Investigating officers must not have felt sure of the relevance of Olga's information, as they began identifying possibly the most diverse array of suspects for a crime in the history of the city. The man who found Carlzen's watch, a neighbor of the Goodsells named F.B. Cowden, was arrested and held while stains on his clothing were analyzed; they were not bloodstains, and he was released. The first major suspect was John Featherstone, age forty-five, a one-eyed black man who was arrested on

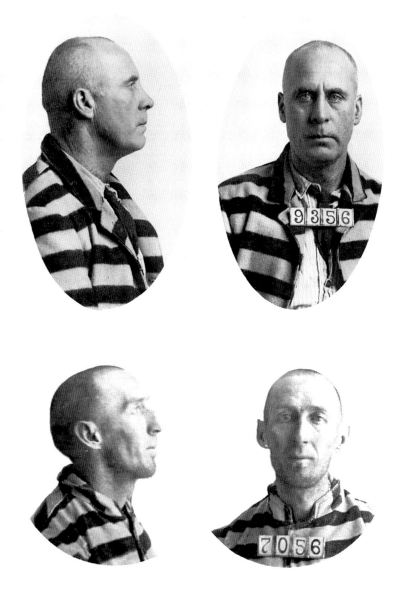

Two of the suspects in Signe Carlzen's murder: wife murderer John Freeze (top) and sex offender Milton Young (bottom). *Colorado State Archives.*

August 14. Featherstone worked for the Robinson Brick Company, half a mile from the crime scene, as a pitman. The foreman discovered a red-stained axe near the brick kilns; the axe belonged to Featherstone. He had at least a partial alibi for the evening, having been at church.

After much media attention, police announced that his axe could not have been the one used in the murder, and Featherstone was no longer a suspect.

On the same day Featherstone was discharged, a new suspect was arrested. "William the Apostle," about seventy years old, was taken into custody on August 14 in Colorado Springs after yelling curses at a group of children. William had been in Denver at the time of Carlzen's murder, and his grip (satchel) contained a bloodstained shirt and handkerchief; he also carried a staff that could have been used as a bludgeon. While the press reported that he matched Olga Kaiser's description, there was actually little or no resemblance. William had drawn attention to himself in Denver—more so than usual—by publicly ranting that barren women were abominations accursed by God and that he had been sent to destroy them. One unfortunate recipient of his lectures was Mrs. H.B. Hall of 702 Julian Street. William knocked on her door, identifying himself as a man of God and begging for food. When she invited him in to eat, "He sat down with us…all the while discussing sexual matters in a most shocking way, and right before my children, too." She noted that William's staff was constructed from a heavy stick thrust into a hollow lead pipe and capped with brass. She was too frightened to throw him out since he appeared to be a "raving maniac."

The other evidence against William was a letter sent to Police Captain John Leyden, containing the statement "when the tree bears no fruit it shall be cut down. Note the word cut and let all parasites of man beware." It was signed "The Sign of the Axe" and ended with a chain letter exhortation to the recipient to copy and send it to nine friends. William refused to provide police with a sample of his handwriting, but the letter was unlikely to have been written by anyone else. And since Carlzen's killer had been determined to be a "degenerate," William's obsession with sex and procreation made him difficult to ignore.

In the meantime, Nick Adams, age fifty-nine, a "deaf and dumb" hobo, was arrested on August 18 at 3236 South Sherman, where he had sought work beating carpets. He had a scratched face and had just written several mysterious annotations on a pillar of the porch. Police concluded that the latter were "hobo signs" advising Adams's peers that the house was "no good" since the owners required work for food. Adams was a petty criminal, and his frequent sign-writing had worried the neighborhood into thinking that their homes were meant for robbery or destruction. However, he could not be placed in Montclair. Similarly, William (whose surname seems never to have been determined) could not be linked to the crime by any evidence other than his eccentricity.

The search for the killer continued. On August 18, the body of a man was found in a room at 1828½ Larimer Street; he had what appeared to be week-old bruises and scars on his chest, arms and face. A memorandum book in his pocket bore the name R.C. Ray and an address in Vincent, Texas. The coroner ruled his death a suicide by inhaling fumes from a gas jet. Unsurprisingly, he did not fit Olga's description, but a shirt blotched with washed-out bloodstains and a coat with a crumpled piece of sheet music in the pocket were among his effects. Carlzen's family could not link the music to their daughter. The man was about fifty-five years old, white and had at least one small puncture wound on his face. A friend of Ray's soon informed police that Ray had died two months ago and that he remained unidentified. Olga was brought in to view the body and declared that he was not the man she saw near the murder site.

The last major suspect arrested in the weeks after the crime was well known to press and police. Milton Young, age forty-four, who seems to have been the usual suspect when a sex crime occurred, was arrested on August 19. A skinny white man with protruding ears and bad teeth, Young worked as a porter and had just been released from prison after serving a four-year sentence for assaulting young girls. First arrested in 1899 on Sixteenth Street after following women who were walking past the post office, Young received the nickname "Jack the Chaser" and a $100 fine (suspended because he was "wrong in his head"). In 1901, he was arrested for assaulting Lena Hegg, age eleven, and Hattie Stillman (aka Stedman), age thirteen. However, neither girl could identify him as her assailant. In October of the same year, Young was caught offering Hulda Scott, age seven, a quarter to accompany him into an alley. He was apprehended, but it does not appear that he was charged for the offense. Eventually, Young wound up in prison; on February 25, 1908, he received a nine- to ten-year sentence for taking "indecent liberties." Released in May 1911, he was free at the time of Carlzen's murder.

Young was, however, most interested in prepubescent girls. If he had attacked Carlzen, it would have been totally out of character. Olga also ruled out Young as the man she saw. There was an attempt to link Carlzen's case to those of other women who had been robbed in the vicinity of the Fourth Avenue car line, but no connection could be established. Police, not being accustomed to lengthy investigations, lost hope rapidly. After three months and the arrest and release of more than twenty-five suspects, the search for the killer was abandoned.

Two years went by without further developments in the case. In 1914, John Freeze, age fifty-two, a former insurance salesman, was charged with the murder of his common-law wife of fourteen years, Rachel (née Lang). Rachel lived at 321 St. Paul Street. Freeze was under court order to stay away from her house. On June 19, 1914, he broke a window, entered the house and shot Rachel in front of their son, Clyde, age six. He told Clyde to call the neighbors and then went into the next room, where he shot himself twice. Rachel had long refused to reconcile with him.

Freeze's picture appeared in the *Rocky Mountain News* during his trial. Olga Kaiser happened to see it and alerted her mother—here was the man she had seen at the Carlzen crime scene. When police were informed, a new flurry of activity commenced. "That Freeze was a degenerate was proved in his recent trial," stated District Attorney John Rush. Moreover, during the days before the Carlzen murder, Freeze and his wife had separated. He was out of work, without a place to live and sleeping outdoors. Clearly, he was without an alibi. A physical examination revealed a number of old scars on his body, some similar in size and shape to hatpin wounds.

Freeze was tried for first-degree murder of Rachel and found guilty. He wept when sons Clyde and Fremont, age eight, testified against him, and he spoke emotionally about his wife's "kindness and sympathy." He had not meant to shoot her—he came to the house to see her one more time before he committed suicide, "then my mind went blank." (This scenario, already a cliché by then, did not help his insanity defense.) Other statements, including the fact that he "felt a great weight lifted from my shoulders" after he shot Rachel, were not likely to have gained the jury's sympathy. He chuckled audibly when he was sentenced to life in prison in November 1914, though "I would not have cared much if they had voted to hang me. You can't do much to hurt a man, after he has once made up his mind that life isn't worth living."

Freeze denied responsibility for Carlzen's death. Perhaps because he was already expected to spend the rest of his life at Canon City, the investigation of his connection to Carlzen's death seems to have been dropped. As of the 1930 census, Freeze was still in prison in Canon City at the age of sixty-eight, and needless to say, Carlzen's death remains a mystery.

Chapter 6

Disturbance of Mind

The following cases involve crimes prompted by mental illness. It is worth noting that the Colorado State Insane Asylum in Pueblo (now renamed the Colorado Mental Health Institute, first opened in 1879) restricts access to patient records, regardless of the age of the documents. Accordingly, it is difficult to verify the details in news reports or to supplement them with dates of release, escape or readmission. Denver was remarkable for its large number of murder-suicides (referred to periodically as an "epidemic" in the local press), which some physicians attributed to the effects of altitude.

Surprisingly, several early twentieth-century Denver murder cases included anti–Christian Science sentiment; they might reflect in exaggerated form the general uneasiness the practitioners inspired among allopathic physicians, public health and child protection advocates and those who disliked mystical spirituality or female self-assertion.

KATE MENIER

"She had often been troubled with hearing people talk about her and seeing them follow her."

On September 3, 1903, Mrs. Lillian Kruse (née Stull), age thirty, was shot and killed at her home at 950 West Seventh Street. Lillian was the wife of Theodore Kruse, a bookbinder at Merchants' Publishing. The shooter was Mrs. Kate Menier (née Flaherty, aka Kate Bernardine), age thirty-five, a fellow bookbinder at the same company. According to the *Denver Post*, Lillian was well regarded in her community: "The neighbors were unequivocal in their praise of the woman who lay dead. She was always so quiet, they said, always refrained from meddling with other people's affairs. They had not been told the reason for the killing, but none of them would admit that it could have been any fault of Mrs. Kruse."

The crime occurred when Menier arrived at the Kruse home, where Lillian was caring for her eight-month-old baby, and knocked at the front door. When Lillian answered, Menier shot her through the screen door with a .32-caliber revolver. Near-eyewitnesses to the murder included Kruse's neighbors, Mrs. Lucy Andrews and Mrs. Christina Peterson. Peterson had

> *gone inside for a bottle of medicine for Mrs. Andrews, who had a headache, when the strange woman in black came down Eleventh Avenue from the east. She stepped up to the door and rapped, but Mrs. Andrews was not looking when the shot was fired. When she heard the report of the revolver and turned again, the woman was running around the corner, and Mrs. Kruse, choking with blood, which was pouring from her mouth and nose, had unlatched the screen door and called to her: "Come over here, quick!"*

The bullet had struck Lillian in the chest; her pulmonary artery was severed, and she died in a few moments. Menier fled, throwing the revolver over a fence; a witness captured her.

When she was apprehended, Menier denied the crime. She was unable to speak coherently about her possibly deceased husband, James Menier, and gave Bernardine as her surname, saying, "No, I am not married: I never was—Menier? He's dead—he always was dead—as dead as a million other

Kate Menier (left) and the Kruse home (right) after the murder, with interested bystanders.

men who walk about dead—Oh, my head! My head!" As she was questioned by Police Chief Hamilton Armstrong, she talked "of what God had done for her." She added, "He gave me the name Bernardine—God gave me that—He gave me more—Oh, the pain—here across my forehead—it throbs all the time—for years it has ached."

Menier had been obsessed with Theodore Kruse. He reported that she had been following him and attempting to gain entry to his house. The day before the shooting, she had been to the house, and Lillian had refused to admit her. "Oh she is crazy," Theodore told reporters. "Only yesterday she was laying for me at Fifteenth and Arapahoe, and last night she was after me with a gun. I dodged into a saloon and slammed the door in her face and got away through the back. Oh, she is crazy." Surprisingly, he did not immediately contact the police about the incident. "Oh, I wish I had asked the chief to arrest her."

On December 10, 1903, Menier was adjudged insane by a jury in the county court. On the stand, Dr. Pershing, an expert on insanity, declared that she suffered from paranoia and was "afflicted with a religious mania. She told him that she could see the angels in heaven and that she had often been troubled with hearing people talk about her and seeing them follow her."

Frank Senter

"She made his home a regular orphan asylum."

Eleanor Senter (née Everett) was eager to embrace the possibilities of the twentieth century and beyond. Writing on December 31, 1900, at 11:45 p.m., she sent greetings to her "grandchild—or great-grandchild, or even great-great-great something" describing her life and requesting "if you enjoy reading this letter from the past to write one for yourselves for the children of the next century, and enclose it with this, not to be opened until the year 2001—just as the year 2000 is going out and 2001 is coming in. Love be with you all." The letter is terribly sad in light of the events a few years later. On February 18, 1904, Frank G. Senter, age fifty-five, a former Rock Island brakeman, went to the residence of his wife, Eleanor, age forty-one, and children at 1322 West Eleventh Avenue to discuss the divorce proceedings that she had initiated. Eleanor did not survive the meeting.

Eleanor had first filed for divorce a year earlier, but the judge declined to grant it to her based on the evidence of erratic behavior that her husband

Eleanor and Frank Senter.

presented. She, however, refused to live with him, and several months before the event, she had filed again for divorce. On the eighteenth, Frank entered the house by the back door and found Eleanor cleaning the bathroom. He tried to get their youngest child, Gano, age thirteen, to leave the house, but the boy was suspicious and refused. Frank asked Eleanor to reconcile with him; she did not want to speak to him and told him to contact her attorney. This angered Frank, and he pulled out a .38-caliber revolver and shot at Eleanor, missing twice, and then he grabbed her and placed the muzzle of the gun against her head for the third shot. Finally, he turned the gun to his own head and fired. Gano witnessed the shooting; he ran from the house and gave the alarm. Both of the Senters died before authorities arrived on the scene.

Eleanor appears to have been energetic and good-hearted, though not in a way guaranteed to impress all of her contemporaries. News coverage was much in Frank's favor; the *Post* and *Times* noted that he had been "driven to insanity by the erratic conduct of his wife" and that the "chief cause of the crime is said to be the wife's devotion to Christian Science." In the divorce case, Frank claimed that Eleanor followed street people into saloons to stop them from drinking, followed "cripples" to urge them to allow her to administer treatment and attempted to heal dogs and horses with broken legs. Further, "She made his home a regular orphan asylum by bringing in children from public institutions for the purpose of healing them…[and] had even brought three negro children into the house to 'cure' and had allowed them to associate with their children."

In 1900, Eleanor was employed as a seamstress at the Ouray Indian Boarding School at Leland, Utah. She had kept in touch with many of the students from her time there, and they visited her on occasion in Denver. Thus another problem, to Frank, was her role in abetting the marriage of Cora Arnold, a Denver society girl, and Alvino Chavarria, a "Santa Clara Indian"; the marriage had been expected since 1900 but only happened in 1907. The couple allegedly met at the Senter home. Eleanor "received some notoriety" as a result. Notoriety was, of course, the last thing Frank wanted.

Frank was also angry with Eleanor's father, Benjamin Everett. Frank had owned some heavily encumbered property in Nebraska that he deeded to his father-in-law. Everett paid off the mortgage and conveyed the property to Eleanor, who sold it to buy the West Eleventh house. A few months later, she mortgaged the house without consulting Frank. Frank had filed suit to have the mortgage set aside. Everett's role in the transaction does not appear especially heinous, but Frank's brief suicide note referred to Eleanor and "Ben Everett, her father, the devil" as the cause of all his troubles. Certainly Everett had made it possible for Eleanor to have her own residence, and that was enough.

Neighbors, on the other hand, blamed Frank for the marital discord, stating that "she could get from her husband no support for herself or her children," so she had been taking in boarders to pay her expenses. He drank and "used exceedingly profane language." Frank had been laid off from his job three weeks earlier. The deaths of Eleanor and Frank Senter left their five children, between the ages of thirteen and twenty-one, orphaned.

On February 7, 1906, the Senter name appeared again in the papers when Frank and Eleanor's eldest son, Frank, then age twenty-three and a salesman and driver for the Palace Bakery, contracted pneumonia. Possibly as a related ailment, he died of a hemorrhagic nosebleed in his room at the Gladstone, at 1641 California Street. Frank reportedly did not seek medical treatment sooner because he was a Christian Scientist. Frank's fiancée, Alice Croft, age twenty-three, learned of his death on February 7. The next day, she engaged a room at 1550 Lincoln Avenue, where she committed suicide by swallowing cyanide of potassium. Newspaper articles suggested that she was not only heartbroken but also penniless and without prospects. As a friend noted, "She expected that when she married her troubles would be over."

In another strange twist, the young witness to the crime, Gano Senter, became a prominent local businessman and a devoted member of the Ku Klux Klan. A typewritten autobiography he composed as an adult merely mentions that his parents died early in his life and then devotes much discussion to his childhood games. This seems incongruous to us today and surely at odds with the detailed news reportage on murder-suicides, but subsequent open discussion of such a family tragedy was probably viewed as unseemly. An amateur psychologist might be tempted to suggest that Eleanor and her enthusiasms were not remembered fondly by the Senter kin, thus providing encouragement for Gano's white supremacist interests. On the other hand, the open and pervasive influence of the KKK in Denver during the 1920s, which has been discussed extensively in other sources, may have been sufficient motivation. In any case, the saga of Frank and Eleanor Senter began with glowing optimism in 1900 and ended with hatred and tragedy.

GEORGE SHISSLER

"Now, damn you! Turn around and take your medicine."

One of Denver's few mass murders took place on March 12, 1905, following the murders of Killian "Key" Sill (aka Fill, a transcription error), age forty-seven, a Denver brick maker, and his wife, Mary L. Sill, age forty-eight, by George Shissler (aka Schistler), age forty-six. Shissler, a Denver teamster and lumberman, lived next door to the Sill residence at Garfield Avenue and Twenty-ninth Street. The subsequent police standoff at the Shissler residence resulted in the deaths of police surgeon Dr. Frank Dulin, age forty-five, and Police Captain William Bohanna, age fifty-one.

Shissler had been arguing with the Sill family over their adjoining properties before deciding to take revenge on them. Key Sill had purchased the property next to Shissler's three years earlier and built a ditch that destroyed Shissler's water rights. The two were not on speaking terms for two years. Then Sill built a line fence between the properties. Shissler tore down the fence, claiming that it was on his land. Sill sued Shissler for damages and prevailed; the damages amounted to about sixty dollars. Shissler brooded about the case for weeks. On March 12, 1905, his family went to church. He remained at home and saw Sill outside at about 11:30 a.m. Shissler approached Sill and yelled, "Now, damn you! Turn around and take your medicine." Sill attempted to flee but was cut down by Shissler's shotgun. Spotting Mary Sill through a window in her house, he shot her as well. He then set fire to their house; their two daughters, Frances, age ten, and Josephine, age fourteen, were in the house at the time but managed to escape. Several news reports noted that one of the Sill children was missing, but this is not reflected in official records.

Shissler then returned to his own home and barricaded himself inside. When the police and ambulances arrived, Shissler began firing. Bystanders helped the ambulance escape as three police wagons surrounded the house. Mayor Robert W. Speer also came to the scene and attempted to approach the house but was driven off with shots.

Some officers volunteered to storm the house to attempt to capture Shissler, dead or alive, but Mayor Speer forbade it. Finally, a policeman caught sight of Shissler's rifle protruding from the bottom of a window and fired. During the course of the action, two men were mortally wounded, police surgeon Dulin and acting chief of police Bohanna. Mike Kelly, a teamster employed by Sill, and several horses were also injured. None of Shissler's other neighbors, however, were wounded in the firefight. When the shooting ceased, Shissler was found dead from gunshot wounds in his bedroom. It was disputed whether his death was from a self-inflicted gunshot

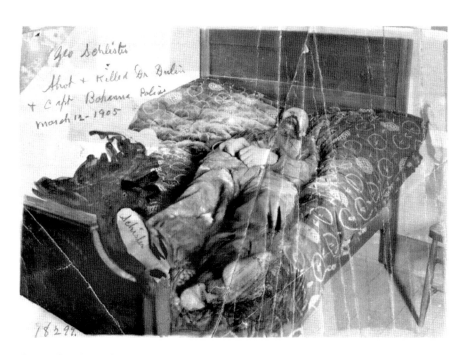

George Shissler in death. *Sam Howe Collection, Colorado Historical Society.*

wound or from police bullets, as he had sustained several wounds on his legs and breast. The coroner's verdict was that the cause of death was a self-inflicted gunshot wound to the head.

His wife and children were at church at the time of the murders; upon their return, reports claim that Mrs. Shissler "fell prostrate. It is thought she will die from shock." Reports note that Shissler was widely regarded as a "maniac" and a man with a querulous disposition whose behavior had worsened in recent years. The *Colorado Transcript* concluded that "the true theory of the cause of his terrible acts seems to be that he had worked himself into a rage and had decided that blood only would satisfy his craving for revenge." Another perspective was provided by the *Daily News*, which averred that Shissler was highly respected by most of his neighbors, "although there have been stories repeated in the neighborhood about his cruelty to his wife and children" and "except when angry he always treated his wife and children with consideration." Judge J.I. Mullins of the district court had ruled in Sill's favor in the fence case and commented, "He was plainly mad, and so anxious to kill every one at all connected with his little lawsuit that I feel as though he would have taken a peculiar delight in shooting me… All through the trial he impressed me as a meek, gentle man. If anyone was aggressive, it seemed to be Sill. I should sooner have expected Sill to have done the shooting than Shissler."

EMILY POWELL

"In the name of the so-called Mrs. Alley I hereby curse Christian Science."

On December 9, 1919, Emily Lippincott Powell, age thirty-eight, shot and killed her ten-year-old daughter, Jacqueline, at their residence, a family hotel at 1000 Corona Street. Four hours later, after writing three notes, Emily shot herself.

Eugene Scobey, a butler, discovered the tragedy when he arrived at the room with a breakfast tray. According to his testimony at the coroner's inquest:

> *About five minutes to 9 I went up to Mrs. Powell's room with a breakfast tray. I knocked and heard her turning over in bed. I knocked again and she asked, "What is it," and I answered "Your breakfast, ma'am," and then she opens the door a little and I shoved it open the rest of the way with my elbow. I saw all the blood. "What's the*

matter?" I asked. "I guess I am crazy," she said to me, "I killed my daughter and shot myself." I ran out to the bannister and called Mrs. Currens [the proprietor] *to come quick.*

Police were summoned immediately. Dr. Samuel Goldhammer, police surgeon, testified that "we found on entering the room a woman with a ragged gunshot wound across her forehead and in another bed was the dead body of a child. The girl had been dead some time. I removed the woman to the hospital. She appeared devoid of feeling and made no statement to me."

Mrs. Eleanor Turner Currens also testified and seemed to have been unfamiliar with the sound of gunshots: "It was after midnight—half an hour after—that I heard several noises in Mrs. Powell's room, which is directly above mine. I thought she had dropped an electric iron. I thought I heard three distinct sounds. Afterwards, I heard her walking around dragging things, and I wondered if she could be packing a box." In fact, Emily fired two shots at Jacqueline and three at herself.

Emily was born into a prominent and wealthy family, the daughter of Horace G. Lippincott of Philadelphia. She attended the elite Miss Porter's School and grew up in a world of privilege. She had lived in Denver for the previous decade and was the former wife of Edwin S. (Todd) Powell. Edwin and Emily had eloped in 1905, but their household was largely supported by Lippincott money. The marriage was unhappy, and the couple divorced

Jacqueline Powell (left) and Emily Lippincott Powell (right).

in 1908. They had two children, son Horace and daughter Jacqueline (who was born after the divorce was granted). At the time of the shooting, Edwin was working in San Francisco as a seller of sporting goods. His mother, Mrs. Elizabeth Powell, did not expect him to come to Denver after the tragedy. She noted that "he has never cared to have me mention the name of his wife and I have never talked to him about his family. He has put her out of his life and this affair probably will not interest him." She also acceded to the desire of the Lippincotts to take her grandson, Horace, age thirteen and a boarder at St. Stephens School in Colorado Springs, to Philadelphia, saying, "He is too young to understand and there will be no need of his being brought here."

Emily's notes were peculiar and revealing. The first was written on the back of a photo of Mrs. W.N. Alley of Chicago, who had lived at the Corona Street hotel about a month before the shooting. It read:

> *All my life my love and my prayers have been thrown back at me. Maybe with my death my curses will be heard. In the name of the so-called Mrs. Alley I hereby curse Christian Science. May every one of them in the universe be stricken with some loathsome disease and all their churches rock and totter from the foundations, and cursed be the hand that shall destroy this picture and the paper that will not publish her fake Christian Science face and this curse.—Emily L. Powell*

According to some reports, Mrs. Alley was only slightly acquainted with Emily and had seldom spoken with her; moreover, she had attended the Congregational church in Denver and was not a believer in Christian

Emily Powell's note, with photograph of Mrs. Alley on the other side.

Science. Mrs. Alley, when asked to comment, expressed puzzlement: "I am sure she doesn't mean me, because I believe I was the best friend Mrs. Powell had…Other guests in the house did not associate with Mrs. Powell, chiefly because she was always complaining of ailments."

Before the murder, Emily had a firm belief that her son, Horace, had died. Her second note, written on blue notepaper, read as follows:

> *I wish before I died I might have known who I am and what has always been wrong with my life. The more I loved people the more I always hurt them. Perhaps had I been more clever I could have found where the fault lay. My boy is dead and Jacqueline and I are going. If someone would only have told me something! Maybe my death or some atonement I could have made would have saved them, but I do not know. My head and my eyes ached so that I could not think well. I hope my family are all well and happy and that I have not hurt them, for I have never been well or happy. May God take Jacqueline's soul. He has my boy's.—Emily L. Powell*

Emily was apparently a heavy smoker. The *Post* reporter noted that her nails and fingers were stained a deep brown, and tobacco was offered as an explanation or symptom of her emotional distress. Mrs. Powell, not an unbiased source, called Emily an "extremist" and described some of her behavior: "She nearly rode a horse to death when just a girl. She would drink nine cups of coffee in succession. I believed that something would happen to her, but I did not think that she would take our Jackie away from us." Emily's brothers, Rowland and George Lippincott, arranged for her transfer to Philadelphia. She left Denver under guard on January 8, 1920. She was adjudged insane by a Philadelphia lunacy commission and confined at Friends Hospital, where she remained for the rest of her life. Emily died on July 14, 1943, and was survived by her son, Horace.

Abner Graves

"One of us had to go."

Abner Graves, age ninety, killed his wife, Minnie (née Latham), age forty-seven, on June 16, 1924. Graves, born in Cooperstown, New York, was known for his involvement in the early days of baseball, including his participation in laying out the baseball diamond where the first game was played. He is still credited

Abner Graves.

as the identifier of Abner Doubleday as the inventor of baseball—a claim that will probably be disputed to the end of time. In any event, Abner Graves had a long life and diverse experiences. He was a pioneer in gold rush California, a Pony Express rider and a mining engineer. At the time of the murder, he had been living in Denver for thirty years and was in poor health. On the occasion of his ninetieth birthday, Graves spoke to reporters optimistically: "I fully expect to live to be 135 years old. And there is no reason why I shouldn't. All my life I have worked hard out in the open…I feel almost as fit and hearty now as I did fifty years ago." He celebrated by "smoking five cigars before nightfall and consuming four cups of coffee."

His second marriage to the much-younger Minnie was of fifteen years' duration (undertaken when Graves was seventy-five and Minnie thirty-three). However, it was not a happy one. The murder occurred when the couple quarreled because Minnie would not sign a bill of sale to their home at 1535 Logan Street. Abner had arranged for a real estate agent to call on them earlier that evening and was incensed at her refusal. He shot her four times.

A dying declaration from Minnie, taken at the hospital, explained her side of the story: "He was quarrelsome during the evening and as he had a quick temper I didn't cross him. He wanted me to sign a bill of sale for our home but I refused." When she brought him a drink, he accused her of putting poison in it. "When I tried to quiet him he jerked out the gun and fired." She asked the assistant district attorney, who was recording her statement, to draw up a new will disinheriting Graves. He did so, and she signed it before lapsing into unconsciousness. She died shortly thereafter.

Abner, unable to walk without crutches, was carried out of the house by police. His stomach was pumped on the chance that he had been poisoned, but none was found. He was questioned by police and related the poisoning story. "So I had to do it," he groaned. "One of us had to go." He was admitted to the mental ward in the county hospital, and a jury shortly thereafter judged him to be insane. He was committed to the state asylum in Pueblo and died there on October 4, 1926.

Chapter 7

Bad Kids

As noted by Wilbur Fiske Stone in his *History of Colorado* (1918), the state enacted its first juvenile law in 1899, providing that "children under sixteen who are vicious, incorrigible or immoral in conduct, or habitual truants from school, or who habitually wander about the streets and public places during school hours or in the night time, having no employment or lawful occupation, shall be deemed disorderly persons, subject to the provisions of the act."

As a practical matter, crimes involving juvenile males in this time period were most frequently property-related. Homicides were relatively few, but they almost invariably involved a dispute with peers and the possession of weapons. Bad boys who were unlucky might arrive in one of two places, depending on age. The Colorado State Reformatory at Buena Vista, established in 1891, housed prisoners on indeterminate sentences depending on good behavior. Prisoners from the state penitentiary could be transferred there if they were between the ages of sixteen and thirty. The State Industrial School for Boys at Golden, for boys between the ages of six and sixteen (though they could be held until age twenty-one), was designed to provide manual training for boys sentenced for truancy or juvenile delinquency.

Girls were arrested most frequently on what we might call morals charges; waywardness might encompass anything from speaking to men on the street to visiting dance halls to prostitution. In March 1898, the *Post* noted, "Hardly a day passes without a report of some girl of tender years suddenly quitting her home and disappearing from sight altogether"; however, the concern was more for the "annoyance to police" than for the girls themselves. An example given in the article was that of Edith Hughey, age fifteen, of 1610 Blake Street: "Edith runs around the streets, holds conversations with men and boys, and does not return home untill [*sic*] late at night. The mother thinks her daughter's waywardness should be curbed by a sentence in the state home." Edith was arrested and charged with being incorrigible, though she "insists her mother keeps her confined in the house too closely." The "Epidemic of Runaway Girls" (a headline in the *News* in 1901) reflected the more restrictive conditions imposed on girls, as well as the more zealous behavioral policing of females.

Bad girls could expect to be charged as incorrigibles and sent to one of the two facilities for delinquent girls, the State Industrial School for Girls (for girls under eighteen with no home or means of support or identified as uncontrollable) or the Home of the Good Shepherd. As discussed here, Denver's juvenile court, the brainchild of controversial judge Benjamin Barr Lindsey, helped to modify attitudes about "incorrigible" juveniles.

BAD BOYS

"The Modern Fagins"

Gangs of boys who committed property crimes, usually in connection with an adult "fence," were fairly common. In 1905, the problem seemed especially prevalent. "Boy Criminals Numerous, Say Denver Police," read one headline in the *Post*. Detective Sam Howe was quoted as stating, "Do you know that nearly all the criminals in Denver today are boys whose ages range between 7 and 21 years?" For example, in June of that year, a gang, allegedly under the control of junk dealer Edward Brown, operated out of his business at 2942 Lafayette Street. Seven boys, ranging in age from eleven to fifteen, stole lead pipe and fittings from vacant houses in the neighborhood; often they would loosen the fittings, and Brown would pick up the material in his wagon later.

Reporters were quick to see parallels to Charles Dickens's *Oliver Twist*. In April 1911, Charles Newman, another junk dealer, was tagged with the nickname "the Modern Fagin." Newman had been found guilty of receiving stolen goods; he used thirteen boys between the ages of nine and sixteen to rifle freight cars and sell him the stolen goods for small sums. Another man dubbed "Fagin" was Marion E. Bush, who managed a gang of boy automobile thieves and was convicted in 1919.

"Innocent Amusements" Gone Awry

Homicides involving boys usually involved fights or what we would call bullying. An early case is simple and typical. On April 29, 1892, Fred Erzgraber, age fifteen and a messenger for the Associated Press, killed Fred Steinmyer, age seventeen. The two were arguing, and the larger Steinmyer attempted to hit Erzgraber with a brickbat. Erzgraber stabbed him in the heart with a pocketknife "with which he had been whittling." He argued self-defense and was acquitted by the jury on December 14.

Of more media interest was the case of Joseph E. Solis, age seventeen, who killed Thomas Devaney, age sixteen. On April 11, 1895, after attending services at the Sacred Heart Church on Twenty-eighth and Larimer, a group of boys began to harass Solis. Solis attempted to flee but was followed by a pack led by Devaney. When Devaney reached him, Solis drew a knife and stabbed Devaney. The victim died on the way to the hospital.

Solis, son of a cigar maker, lived at 2009-15 Arapahoe Street with his parents. He explained that Devaney had called him names (one of which was "Priest"), and then another boy punched him in the nose. Solis went into church for the service, but when he came out, a gang of boys was

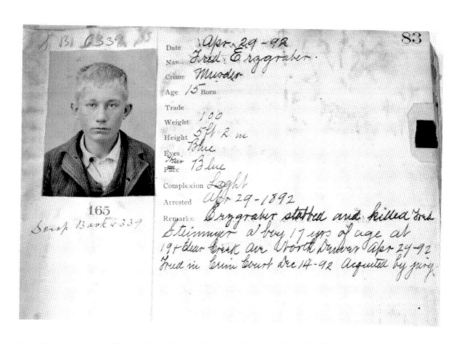

Fred Erzgraber, age fifteen. *Sam Howe Collection, Colorado Historical Society.*

waiting for him. They caught him by the coat and struck him again. Solis "pulled my knife out of my pocket and I tried to protect myself." He claimed he did not know that he had cut Devaney until later.

Solis's story was confirmed by the rest of the boys; he "was the subject of much innocent amusement on the part of the other boys, owing to his nervous temperament." He attended church so frequently that he received his nickname, and this distressed him greatly. Since the other boys admitted the pursuit and attack, they evidently did see it as "innocent amusement" rather than vicious bullying. Nonetheless, the case against Solis was dismissed on the request of the district attorney, who did not believe that the wound was inflicted with malice.

Similar to the Solis case was the February 28, 1898 death of nineteen-year-old John Purcell, the son of a bricklayer, at the hands of Mike Nilan, age fifteen, of 1036 South Seventh Street. The death was the result from a blow with a baseball bat.

The crime occurred near a vacant lot at 1003 South Ninth Street. According to the trial transcript and the testimonies of the other children who were playing alongside Purcell and Nilan, the boys had been sitting on top of a shed along the street. Purcell, reportedly much larger than Nilan, began harassing the latter by throwing a rope over his neck and pulling him from the shed. This caused Nilan's pants to tear, and the other boys laughed. Purcell asked to see the tear, but instead of sympathizing, he tore Nilan's pants further.

Nilan then picked up a baseball bat and threatened to hit Purcell. Purcell mocked Nilan, saying, "If you want to hit me, you know where to find me; you wouldn't hit nothing." (Nilan also claimed that Purcell applied a "vile epithet" to him—"little son of a bitch"—but the other children did not remember the expletive.) Purcell resumed playing with the others but approached Nilan again a short while later. Testimony given by the children is somewhat unclear on the specifics of what followed. As Purcell bent down, either to tie his shoe or to pick up a rock to throw at Nilan, the latter took the opportunity to strike him on the back of the head with the bat. Nilan then ran home, afraid that Purcell would "get up and thrash me." The other children also ran off, frightened, to get help. Purcell was carried to Allen's Drugstore two blocks away, and an ambulance was called. He died two hours later at the hospital.

Nilan was apprehended at his home at 1036 South Seventh Street. He was later released from jail on a $500 bond, which his father, a stonemason, procured. The court proceedings began on April 14. Nilan, who was "an

Michael Nilan and other interested parties.

excellent witness for himself," was described as anything but threatening: "His face was small, freckled, pink, honest and except when he smiled, stupid. There was not the least trace of ill-humor or malice in it. His mein [mien] and manners were those of a rather timid, bullied and shrinking little boy."

Neither Nilan nor his family had believed that he would be convicted. However, when the verdict was rendered two days later, he was found guilty of murder in the second degree. An appeal to the Colorado Supreme Court brought about a reversal of the judgment in January 1900 on the grounds that the jury had held Nilan to a higher standard (that he had to be in fear for his life) than was required (being justifiably in fear of assault/battery and using reasonable means to prevent the attack). Nilan does not appear to have been re-tried.

In general, courts were unwilling to impose harsh sentences on the defendants in these ambiguous cases. A final example is Albert Thorman, age fourteen, who shot Gustavus "Gus" Roeghan, age twenty, on October 21, 1901, near Akron in Arapahoe County. Preexisting ill-feeling may have been a cause, but the precipitating incident was the intrusion of Thorman's cattle onto disputed property. Thorman claimed that Roeghan raised a heavy whip to strike him; the former had a Winchester rifle with him and fired. Allegedly, the "ball struck Roghan squarely in the heart, tearing it almost out of his body. As he reeled from the saddle, Thorman fired again, the second shot tearing off one side of his head."

Thorman claimed self-defense during his trial in the West Side Court but was still convicted of voluntary manslaughter. He was sentenced to fourteen months at the State Industrial School in Golden but was released in August 1902 after only nine months. Reportedly, there were complaints that Thorman's release was against the policy of the institution (to release a boy only when his mandatory sentence was up); the State Industrial School gave no explanation for the early release.

The Jesse James Gang

One of the most interesting juvenile cases in Denver concerns the August 12, 1901 shooting death of twelve-year-old Homer Reahard, allegedly at the hands of eight young boys known as the Jesse James Gang. The murder occurred after an argument between Reahard and the group of young boys while Reahard was tending to his family's livestock on the edge of town near Third and Alcott Street. Reahard's body was discovered after he failed to return home for dinner that day. A doctor was quickly summoned, but the young boy died soon afterward.

It was initially believed that Reahard's death was the result of a hunting accident, but two detectives, Connor and McNeill, arrested the eight young men after a private detective hired by Reahard's father, James, learned details of the murder from a young boy named Leonard Haley, age ten. The boys arrested in connection with the murder were Casey Gaul, age twelve; Sam Gaul, age fourteen; Chester "Chet" John, age fourteen; Ray Pool (aka Poole), age fourteen; George W. Brune, age fourteen; Charles Brune, age fourteen; Roy Brune, age twelve; and Henry Brune, age nineteen.

All of the boys in question underwent extensive questioning before Casey Gaul, the youngest of the group, confessed. Gaul described the events leading up to the murder:

> *Charlie* [Brune] *called Homer a* ------ [expletive deleted in original]. *They started fighting and then George Brune pitched on and Homer licked both of them. Then Roy Brune said he'd fight Homer alone, and Homer licked him. Then Henry Brune kicked Homer in the stomach and Chet John kicked him; and then little George Brune hit him in the side with a*

The only available image of Homer
Reahard as he appeared around the
time of the shooting.

*rock as big as a base ball, and then Roy Brune went over and sat down
under a tree and I kicked Homer on the soles of his shoes as he was lying
down. He begged us not to kill him. After Homer had licked the Brunes
he was tripped by Poole and fell on his back, then rolled over on his face,
putting both hands up to his face. Ray Poole pulled his gun out and says:
"Here goes!" Henry Brune tried to stop Ray, but Ray shot Homer before
Henry could do anything. He shot three times, I think.*

One bullet struck Homer in the head. Leonard Haley, the boy who spoke
with the detective, saw the incident; the boys told him not to say anything
or they would kill him. The boys allegedly had a grudge against Homer
"because he would not let Chet play ball" the week before. On September
13, after Gaul's confession, three more members of the Jesse James Gang
confessed to being present when Ray Pool shot Reahard.

However, not long after this, Gaul repudiated his confession, telling
authorities that "he had hatched up the story implicating Pool, believing it
would be the means of securing his own release from prison." However, both
Pool and Gaul remained in jail, allegedly because the judge presiding over
the case believed that Reahard's father might kill them. Pool commented,
"It's a lie, and Casey had no right to tell it."

The Jesse James Gang, with notations by Detective Sam Howe. *Left to right*: Chester John, Charles Brune, Roy Brune, Casey Gaul (front), Henry Brune, George Brune, Ray Pool (front) and Sam Gaul. *Sam Howe Collection, Colorado Historical Society.*

The criminal trial of the Jesse James Gang began on October 26, 1901. According to the *Colorado Transcript*, "The contention of the prosecution [was] that the boys now facing the jury are members of an organization of youngsters banded together for the purpose of emulating in a small way the deeds of dime novel heroes." This was seconded by the *Longmont Ledger*: "Colorado has a deplorable sensation in the shape of a set of eight boys, calling themselves the 'Jesse James' gang. The killing of Homer Reahard shows to what extent such an organization of boys will lead to. The reading of tough literature is said to be one of the causes which led to the forming of the band...It is discouraging to lovers of law and order that such boys are growing up in Colorado. Of course, they will help fill the reformatory, but there is not much satisfaction in that." Another story about Reahard's alleged killers ran with the headline, "James Gang Had a Cave Where They Persecuted Small Boys."

The youngest boys were tried first—Roy, Charles and George Brune and Casey Gaul—and they were charged with murder. The boys claimed to have been swimming at the time of the homicide, and all denied any knowledge of the circumstances of Homer's death. Another boy, Ray Caldwell, age fourteen, testified in support of the alibi. Casey, though nervous, maintained that his confession was coerced and that he had been struck on the head by an officer; Roy Brune, age ten and the youngest defendant, also claimed to have been hit on the head and legs by police. Two women testified to seeing Ray Pool near the scene of the crime at the time of the murder, when he claimed to have been far from the scene; defense counsel suggested that they were confused about the date of the encounter.

Public opinion began to shift during the trial. One headline declared, "Babies Face Jury on Charges of Murder." Furthermore, one commentator noted, "People say: 'Isn't it awful?' but they don't know anything about the awfulness of it, unless they have seen the scared, miserable boys, and the white drawn faces of their mothers." He further commented upon the conditions the accused boys were living in while in jail. "It is a disgrace in Denver. There ought to be a clean, light, decent place for prisoners, and a place of detention for those held as witnesses, instead of herding them all in together and punishing the suspect as if he were already a convicted felon."

In the end, a verdict of assault and battery (a far cry from first-degree murder) was returned against Roy, Charles and George Brune and Casey Gaul on November 18. Under the terms of the verdict, they were to be sent to the county jail for six months or to the state reform school until they were twenty-one years old. There was no mention of the outcome of the trials of Chet John and Henry Brune, although it was mentioned that Ray Pool was released for lack of evidence after being held in jail for two months. The three Brune brothers and Casey Gaul were released for good behavior after six months and returned to their homes. Further, it was argued that "since the court had discharged the principal in the case, Ray Poole…it was not right to detain these four."

The Brune brothers, Henry (died 1953), Roy (died 1972) and George (died 1971), are buried side by side in Fairmount Cemetery, with a common headstone. All were still living with their parents at the time of the 1930 census (when they were ages forty-five, forty-one and thirty-eight), so it is unlikely they had families of their own. Charles Brune married and was division manager of a grocery store according to the 1940 census; his date of death is unknown. Ray Pool died in 1919, just shy of his thirty-third birthday, in Montrose, Colorado.

Neal Wright, His Mother Berta and Judge Lindsey

It is necessary to mention Judge Benjamin Barr Lindsey, campaigner for reform, gubernatorial candidate and—most importantly for our purposes—the creator of Denver's juvenile court. Lindsey was a tireless advocate for the protection and rehabilitation of child offenders. He was an odd combination of outspoken altruism and self-aggrandizement, and it is not surprising that he was both respected and vilified.

In his autobiographical collection *The Beast* (1910), Lindsey averred:

I had begun merely with a sympathy for children and a conviction that our laws against crime were as inapplicable to children as they would be to idiots...I found—what so many others have found—that children are neither good nor bad, but either strong or weak. They are naturally neither moral nor immoral—but merely unmoral...Our work, we found, was to aid the civilizing forces—the home, the school, and the church—and to protect society by making the children good members of society instead of punishing them for being irresponsible ones. If we failed, and the child proved incorrigible, the criminal law could then be invoked. But the infrequency with which we failed was one of the surprises of the work.

One of the better-known juvenile cases in Denver involved the April 18, 1915 murder of John A. Wright, age forty-two, by either his son, Neal, age twelve, or his wife, Berta, age thirty-two, in their Denver home located at 3350 Adams Street. Wright, a city worker, was shot as he attempted to enter the house; he was intoxicated at the time.

The motive behind the murder was said to be frustration over ongoing conflict between the couple. As one source reported, "According to the woman's story, she could not resist trying to kill Wright after fourteen years of effort on her behalf in attempting to reform the man." She concurred: "For fourteen years I asked myself many questions. When the bills came due on the paydays that never brought me any money, when I worked and toiled and stitched and sewed until the late hours, when that man I had chosen to give my life to came home and cursed me, I became brave and I shot him."

Berta Wright confessed to the murder, but the case became complicated during the trial when Neal stated that it had been he, not his mother, who had shot his father. He had done it to frighten his father, not to kill him. The incident was further complicated when Judge Lindsey was called in to speak with the boy and ascertain the truthfulness of his statement. Lindsey spoke with Neal but refused to divulge any information from his conversations to the court, citing confidentiality. Lindsey was charged with contempt of court, but he refused to violate Neal's confidence. He was fined $500.

Lindsey used the opportunity to state his view, saying, "I would far rather go to jail and rot than to betray the confidence of a child." Berta was acquitted on June 10. However, newspapers routinely and unapologetically referred to Berta as John Wright's killer rather than Neal. They soon had another opportunity to do so: she returned to the news when Mrs. Emma

Mulling, in the process of divorcing husband Leon, a cook, included details of his relationship with Berta (now Mrs. Berta Fay). Mulling neglected his family but went out with Berta at night and bought her a fifty-dollar coat.

Berta's date of death is unknown. Neal Wright, a World War I veteran, died in 1975. Lindsey was ousted from the juvenile court in 1924 by pro-Klan interests. In keeping with his sense of the dramatic, but to the despair of historians, he took his court files to his home at 1343 Ogden Street, shredded them and burned the remnants in a nearby vacant lot. A photographer was present to capture the event.

BAD GIRLS

What Happened to Jessie Kinport?

One of the most intriguing cases involving a teenaged girl could fall into many categories in this book. At first, the case appeared to involve the acts of a madman. The truth, however, was much more complex.

On July 8, 1901, two violent crimes occurred in Denver: the murder of Armina Bullis and the rape of teenager Jessie Kinport. Chris Jensen (full name Christian Jensen, aka Johnson), age thirty, a Danish-born laborer, was arrested for both crimes.

Armina Bullis (aka Armenia or Amenia), age sixty-three, owned a ten-acre ranch on Coronado Avenue in an area then known as Myrtle Hill. This location was near the eastern city limits. The description of Bullis as a property owner is deceptive; she had received the farm in a divorce settlement eight years earlier, and it was scarcely in operation. Her home was an unpainted one-story shack, she kept no stock and the ground was uncultivated. She lived alone, kept chickens and made a living by doing washing in the city, walking back and forth to work.

About a mile and a half from her home, at Exposition and University Avenues, she met with a violent death. An area resident, Mrs. William Sorensen, was out early the next morning to deliver milk. She discovered Bullis's body lying across the "lonely country road," which had obviously seen no traffic overnight. In fact, between that location and Bullis's home, there were no houses, merely prairie and pasture. Bullis had been stabbed to death. By her side was a bundle of scraps for her chickens.

Jensen's second victim, schoolgirl Jessie Kinport, age fourteen, lived at 119 West Ninth Avenue. The Kinports were a respectable, financially

Armina Bullis.

comfortable family. Father Jesse E. Kinport, the "Van Man" of Denver, had a lucrative furniture moving and storage company before his death from typhoid fever in 1899.

Jessie, her mother, Carrie (née Hausling), and her late father's business partner, Thomas Duffy, went out to dinner one night. Carrie and Duffy went on to Elitch's Gardens, while Jessie was escorted home by Allen Fulton, age fifteen. They sat on the porch for a while and talked, and then Fulton departed at 10:30 p.m.

Carrie returned home at 11:00 p.m. She looked into Jessie's room. Jessie was not there, and the bedclothes were stained with blood. She raised an alarm, and police began a search. Jessie was found in a vacant lot about a block from the rear of her home, "clad only in an undergarment." She had been sexually assaulted and claimed to have no recollection of the attack other than being dragged out of her bed, down the stairs and outside the house. Confined to her bed, she was unable to provide further details and was in a state of shock.

Jensen was next seen on the Myrtle Hill streetcar that evening. He was carrying a knife in his hand, and the other passengers became unnerved. A police officer named Lambert happened to be on the car; he had to be prompted to take action, to the annoyance of the civilian passengers (one man commented, "I never saw such cowardice"). Lambert finally began to talk to Jensen, who asked him "how badly had [I] injured the woman?" Lambert, nonplussed, said, "What woman?" Jensen replied, "They were after me with guns, I struck her and she yelled pretty good." Lambert asked for the knife, and Jensen obeyed without hesitation. When the car reached Broadway, he was placed under arrest and taken to the police station.

Jensen proved to be marginally coherent when interviewed by police and medical personnel. He stated that he came to the United States at age nineteen and lived in Topeka and Lawrence, Kansas, from that time until he was twenty-seven years old. While in Topeka, he had been shot in a dispute, and his episodes of violence were attributed to what appeared to be epileptic seizures that began in his last two years in Kansas. He left for Colorado, where he worked on a farm and at a sawmill near Glenwood Springs, and then came to Denver about two months before the crime occurred. He readily admitted that he had killed Bullis and attacked Jessie.

A mob began to gather in front of the city jail, and police feared an attack was imminent. On July

Jessie Kinport.

9, Jensen, heavily shackled, was surreptitiously removed to the Colorado Springs County Jail. Jail authorities reportedly "[did] not doubt his sanity" and believed that he was shamming. The medical community, however, disagreed. One doctor opined that the wave of motiveless crimes in Denver was "caused in many cases by the peculiar effect of drugs on persons living in a high altitude…the nervous system of persons in Denver is at a high tension. Now, I can't exactly account for it, but a morphine fiend or a cocaine fiend goes to rack and ruin here quicker than in any place I was ever in."

The July 1903 *Denver Medical Times* featured neurologist Dr. S.D. Hopkins's case study of Jensen, entitled "Homicide Committed While in the Amnesic State." Jensen had been working for Charles Nadler for about three months before the crime. He recalled being taken sick on July 4, running away from two men he called "hold-ups" and then recollecting nothing until he found himself in the county jail in Colorado Springs on July 10. Nadler described Jensen as drowsy and then irritable and agitated in the days between July 4 and 9. Three examining physicians testified that Jensen was suffering from "epileptic amnesia" at the time of the murder and was not criminally responsible for his acts.

It was the only excuse to offer. Jensen's offenses were often compared to the Capitol Hill Slugger's in their excessive violence and apparent pointlessness. The only other theory was argued by Bullis's niece, who claimed that the

Chris Jensen.

victim's ex-husband had paid Jensen to kill her so that he would inherit her ranch. This theory does not appear to have received serious consideration.

The jury agreed with the physicians' insanity assessment. Jensen was sent to the state asylum at Pueblo on July 23. He escaped from the asylum on October 28, 1902, allegedly "by breaking several bars in the front of his cell." If accurate, this report suggests that he remained violent while incarcerated. It was speculated that he might have joined his brother in South Africa, but this was not the case. After five years in the outside world, he resurfaced in September 1907, appearing at Denver police headquarters and asking for food and lodging. He was not immediately recognized and was given temporary shelter in a cell at the city jail. He experienced hallucinations at night and so was interviewed by the police surgeon. He stated that he didn't want to be released because he might kill someone; he was being pursued by "little red devils [but] they don't come into the jail." However, he was released the next morning. He returned to police headquarters in the afternoon, again claiming that he was being chased and wanted to remain in the jail. He was sent away again. Finally, Police Captain Frank Lee remembered Jensen and sent two detectives out to apprehend him. They captured him at Fourteenth and Larimer Streets. He was returned to the Pueblo Asylum on November 7, 1907.

The "double tragedy" of July 8 received a great deal of news coverage. However, some details of Jessie's assault were difficult to understand. Newspapers had reported that Jessie's bed was "blood soaked"; instead, there were only a few spots of blood on her pillow, consistent with a minor nosebleed. Carrie would not allow police to interview Jessie in the days immediately after the crime and did not permit a physical examination either. The path taken to reach Jessie's room suggested an intruder who was acquainted with the house. Finally, the timetable of the events exonerated Jensen; he had been booked in jail at 10:30 p.m., and Jessie's attack took place after that time.

When Jensen was ruled out as the attacker and no other suspect presented himself, police began to look at Jessie's male friends. Carrie unwittingly pointed out a defect in Jessie's story: "Jessie was not a wild girl, but she was thoughtless and careless…I always encouraged her to bring her friends here. It was absolutely impossible for any of her boy acquaintances to choke her and carry her out of the house, for they simply were not large enough. She was as large as they were."

Police applied pressure, and Jessie finally admitted on July 26 that her assailant was Roy Pennington (aka Leroy Pennington), age fifteen, son of John L. Pennington, operator of a saloon at 1745 Curtis. It was thought that Pennington had come to the Kinport house to return a photograph. Arriving soon after Fulton's departure, he was let into the house by Jessie and later attacked her against her will; she ran downstairs after he left and collapsed outside, dazed and hysterical. Jessie, when cautioned about making a false accusation, answered sadly, "Do you think I want to send him to the penitentiary unless he is the one? I used to like Roy." Brought face to face with Pennington at the police station, she sobbed, "You did it, you know you did it. Oh, Roy, why, why did you do it?"

Pennington, of course, denied that he had been anywhere near Jessie that evening, though he claimed that they had "improper" relations previously, on June 10 and 11. Instead, he had been at the Pennington home at 1239 Downing Avenue all evening. His alibi was supported by his parents, his brother, Charles, and a next-door neighbor. They were hardly the most impartial witnesses, but they seemed more credible than Jessie at this point; she acknowledged the earlier sexual episodes with Pennington but claimed duress on those occasions as well. Thus, while Pennington was tried for Jessie's assault, the result was a hung jury and a dismissal of the case on March 2, 1902.

Roy Pennington, the guilty party.

Carrie Kinport bemoaned the public infamy the case had drawn: "We are living under a terrible nervous strain, and this matter should be settled immediately. We have been before the public constantly ever since the night of the assault and, oh, I wish it were over. Some of the newspapers have treated us shamefully, too. In this morning's *Rocky Mountain News* there appeared what purported to be a statement from Jessie, which was a fabrication from beginning to end. There was a not a word of truth in it."

Jessie was reportedly forced to withdraw from Manual High School, based on her notoriety; later, however, she received her degree from the school. Later still, using the name J. Catherine Kinport, she received a teaching certificate from the Colorado State Teachers College (now the University of Northern Colorado), a BA from Columbia University in New York City and a master's degree from the University of Denver. She taught for forty years at Washington Park Elementary School and Byers Junior High School, retiring in 1953. On June 21, 1930, she married Francis Walter Abell; there were no children from the marriage. Abell died in 1971. Jessie died at the age

Charles Pennington and Anastasia Tobin Pennington in Detective Sam Howe's "murder book." *Sam Howe Collection, Colorado Historical Society.*

of ninety in March 1978; she was buried as "Catherine Kinport Abell" with her mother and father at Fairmount Cemetery.

Roy Pennington's siblings also engaged in some newsworthy conduct. On May 2, 1906, his brother, Charles, age twenty-three, struck and killed his common-law wife, Anastasia "Ruby" Tobin Pennington (aka "Babe"), age unknown, a variety actress. Charles was a bartender in his father's saloon. He and Tobin had been living together for four years. The crime took place in a rooming house at 1756 Curtis Street. The Irish-born Tobin was in poor health and "weighed scarcely ninety pounds," while Charles weighed two hundred pounds. According to Charles, "That smack was not hard enough to kill, and I am sure that death was due to her weak heart." He pleaded guilty to involuntary manslaughter and served one day in county jail. Detective Sam Howe was obviously dissatisfied with the verdict, scrawling the word "Rotten" on Charles's entry in the murder book. He also noted that Charles was sent to prison later on another offense and was killed in an accident in 1915 while working on a road gang.

Saved by Marriage

Mabel Manning, age twenty-five, a Denver seamstress and shoplifter, was sent to the state penitentiary in Canon City on January 22, 1911, for a term of two to three years. George A. Reid (aka Reed), age thirty, an Arizona forest ranger who knew Manning when she lived in that state, visited her in prison regularly. He appeared before the state board of pardons and offered to marry Manning upon her release if her sentence were commuted. The *Post* reported that "the board considered this unique proposition favorably." On June 14, the couple were married and left for Arizona.

Actually, Manning's case was far from unique. The fact that she was already in prison was perhaps a novelty, but female offenders—particularly, of course, juveniles—were routinely released from jail if men agreed to marry them. In some cases, the groom was a paramour/seducer associated with the girl and in others a noble rescuer like George Reid.

On December 14, 1901, the *News* announced a happy resolution to the cases of two runaway girls: cousins Elsie Coltrin (aka Colton) and Pearl Williamson, both age sixteen. The police were notified and began a search: "It was said that two young men inspired the girls to run away from their homes." As it turned out, they had indeed fled to Loveland (appropriately) with two young men. All the parties met with the girls' parents at the police station, where the matter was resolved by obtaining marriage licenses; Coltrin

Mabel Manning. *Colorado State Archives.*

would wed Lyman E. Hamilton of St. Louis, Missouri, and Williamson would wed Fred W. Howing, also of St. Louis. The paper noted that by doing so, the girls had "stopped all proceedings to punish them."

On April 10, 1905, May Cunningham, age fourteen, was arrested in a Lawrence Street rooming house with George A. Bishop, age unknown. Cunningham's mother had been in the Pueblo Asylum for the previous five years, and her father left her in the care of Mattie Tripp of 2302 Larimer Street. According to Cunningham, Bishop was the best of a bad lot of choices: "I was just driven to it. My father does not pay for my support, and Mrs. Tripp, who has been caring for me, was trying to make me lead an immoral life. This boy offered to take me, so I just went with him." The next day, the *Post* followed up on the story. Cunningham and Bishop were swiftly married:

> *The father, John Cunningham, a coal miner at Leyden, was sent for by Chief of Police Delaney. The matter was laid before him and he was advised to give his consent to his daughter's marriage. "What!" he shouted. "I would rather see her dead." He was calmed down and both the chief and Humane Agent Oliver Tuft told him it was the best thing to do, and he finally consented.*

There was no mention of any further investigation of Mrs. Tripp or of Mr. Cunningham's abandonment of his daughter. The problem was considered solved. This is all the more surprising because Mattie Tripp was known to police. In 1893, she was operating a "den" at 1446 Larimer Street where two runaway girls, ages fifteen and sixteen, were found in a bedroom with three men.

If the marriage option failed, a bad girl might find herself irrevocably disgraced. In December 1896, Addie Krapf (aka Daisy), an orphaned teenaged girl, was confined at the State Industrial School. The man who "ruined" her, a married man named William "Al" Morehead, was facing a felony charge in connection with his actions toward Krapf. He was released on bail and obtained a divorce. The felony charges against him were continued, "it being understood that the girl was to be released from the reform school and they would be married and the charges against him would be dropped." However, reported the *Aspen Weekly Times*, "Miss Krapf knocked the pardon scheme in the head by her absolute refusal to marry Al Morehead, her seducer, or to have anything to do with him." The recommended pardon was revoked, and Krapf remained at the school.

Another incident seems particularly sordid. On January 10, 1906, five young males between the ages of sixteen and twenty-three were charged with statutory rape for engaging in sexual activity with Anna Hudson, age sixteen, in dugouts or caves in a vacant lot at Santa Fe and West Twelfth Avenue. The caves were also used to hide stolen goods. The boys—George

The cave at Santa Fe and West Twelfth Streets, with beer keg visible.

Anna Hudson and the boys in a photomontage from the *Denver Times*. *Left to right*: Philip J. Toner, John Dixon, George Downing, John Bartz and John Summers.

Downing, age eighteen; Philip J. Toner, age sixteen; John Bartz, age sixteen; John Dixon, age eighteen; and John Summers, age eighteen—had, according to Hudson, enticed other girls into the caves as well and provided kegs of beer for what the *News* called "libidinous orgies."

Hudson, a bakery worker, had essentially been abandoned by her mother, Dillie Hudson. Further, it was "charged by police that Dillie Hudson held improper relations with the same young men that came to see her daughter." Hudson earned very little money at her job and relied on the money she received from the boys. Her father was dead, and her young brothers were in the Denver Orphans' Home.

The *Aspen Democrat* revealed that Hudson had been married to George Fleming, age nineteen, on October 27, 1905. Fleming had been a member of the cave group as well. Then, "on the investigation of the juvenile court two months ago Fleming realized the wrong which he had done the girl, offered to marry her and on her consent the ceremony was performed by a justice of the peace." However, Hudson left Fleming and went back to her old life. Perhaps both parties viewed the marriage as no more than a formality to avoid legal repercussions.

On January 24, at the preliminary hearing of the boys who had "wrecked" her life, Hudson "broke down on the witness stand. She wept bitterly and could not be made to tell the most vital part of the story."

The White Slaves of Denver

Bessie Hunt, age unknown, and Margaret Reibold (aka Riebold), age nineteen, were accused of leading Nellie Graham (aka Ward), age fifteen, "the daughter of respectable parents," into a life of shame. Hunt was the landlady/madam of a house at 2052 Market Street. In contrast, Graham's respectable family lived on West Thirty-fourth Avenue. She told an almost archetypal story of entrapment. She wanted to earn some money, so she took a job at the National Biscuit Factory on Blake Street: "Some of the girls in the factory talked bad and I did not like them at first, but they always had money to spend and were good to me." One day in January 1906, Reibold told Graham that she knew of an easier way to make money than factory labor and offered to take her to this place. Graham demurred, and Reibold soon quit the factory. She had, however, introduced Graham to a young man named Buster Moore.

One day, Graham was walking along Larimer Street when she encountered Moore. He offered to escort her to see Reibold. Once at Market Street, Graham did not want to enter the house but was convinced to do so because Reibold was not dressed to go out. Hunt and Reibold "took me into a room and talked to me for a long time. They told me that I would make lots of money and would never have to work again. I said no, and Bessie Hunt said that I would have to stay whether I wanted to or not." Graham was locked in a room and watched constantly. "At night time men came to the house and they would send some of them into the room with me." She eventually escaped but was ashamed to go home, so she went to "Lou Belmont's place," another brothel located at 1955 Market (and also referred to as "Lou Dillon's" in the space of the same news story), where she was promised, allegedly, no men in her room. Alas, "they treated me just the same as they did at the other house. The policeman found me there and arrested me. I want to go home, and if my mother will forgive me I will never run around with bad girls anymore."

Graham's story was not very convincing. She had apparently told her mother that she had to work nights at the factory (which implies that she was home in the day). When she did not return after one night, her sister was sent to the factory to inquire after her and found that she had not been working

Bessie Hunt (left) and Margaret Reibold (right).

there. She could not have expected the second brothel to treat her differently than the first. Also, the mention of "the policeman" means that she was probably arrested for prostitution. In spite of her account, her mother had her committed to the House of the Good Shepherd.

A similar story was told by Elsie May Chesley, age fifteen. On January 3, 1913, Chesley, a maid, went to the Union depot to take up a similar position in Salida, Colorado. She disappeared from the station. The *Republican* announced that the "juvenile authorities" believed that she had been kidnapped or taken by "white slavers." Chesley turned up three days later with a dubious story that paralleled Graham's in several respects.

According to Chesley, a woman veiled in black approached her, asking if she were Miss Elsie Chesley. When Chesley replied in the affirmative, the woman told her that Chesley's sister, Gladys, who was at the detention home, was very ill and wanted to see her. Chesley accompanied the women to her automobile on Market Street, where the woman pushed her in the car and pressed a handkerchief soaked in chloroform over her face. When she regained consciousness, she was in a small windowless room, clad only in a nightgown. A different veiled woman came to the door and threatened her with a gun, telling her to keep quiet. She was brought food and drink, which must have been drugged, because she slept a great deal. On January 6, the woman brought Chesley her clothes and told her that she would be released, but she had to swear she would not divulge what had happened to her.

The woman gave Chesley some coffee, which again must have been drugged, and she next remembered being dropped off on the corner of Fourteenth and Curtis. She entered a restaurant and was recognized by a waitress, who asked her if she was the girl who had been kidnapped. In a rather complicated and unnecessary maneuver, Chesley borrowed clothes from the waitress, left her own clothes behind as surety and went home. The messenger boy who exchanged the borrowed clothes between the parties later stated that he "thought the whole affair a practical joke." After her return, Chesley was reportedly staying with her sister, Mabel Chesley, at 78 Jackson Street.

Elsie Chesley.

The red flags in the story were obvious. Any references to "the detention home," "Market Street" and veiled women in black should have put Chesley (or her listeners) on guard. Her story is an excellent illustration of the extent to which the "white slavery" problem was used as a shield by some of the alleged victims. A Colorado-born Elsie Chesley of the right age appears in the 1930 U.S. Census. She was married to a contractor named Walter Aldrich and living in Bucksport, California.

Chapter 8

Pecuniary Motives

S everal of the cases summarized previously involved financial gain. This chapter covers the ones that do not fit neatly into the other categories—specifically, murder for insurance proceeds, threats of extortion with explosives, fights over wages and another look at the world of bootlegging.

ANDREW SPUTE

"I wished to make the amount larger for the reason that she intended on a trip east and also intended camping in the mountains."

One unusual case involved Andrew J. Spute, age thirty-five, the Swedish owner of a grocery store located at 1238 Santa Fe Avenue, and his alleged murder of his entire family in a boating accident for insurance money on October 25, 1896, at Smith's Lake (aka Smiths Lake) in Washington Park (located at Virginia Avenue/Downing Street, Louisiana Avenue and Franklin Street).

Spute's wife, Hilda, age unknown, and five children (Evan, age thirteen; Carl, age eight; Edith, age six; and twins Ruth and Esther, seventeen months old) died when their pleasure boat unexpectedly capsized. Spute claimed that his inability to swim prevented him from saving his family, although he was able to save himself. Because there were few witnesses, their deaths were initially regarded as accidental. However, Spute was brought under suspicion when investigators began to examine the $10,000 life insurance policy (issued on August 4, 1896, by Traveler's Insurance Company) carried by his wife. According to witnesses, Hilda had signed the policy documents,

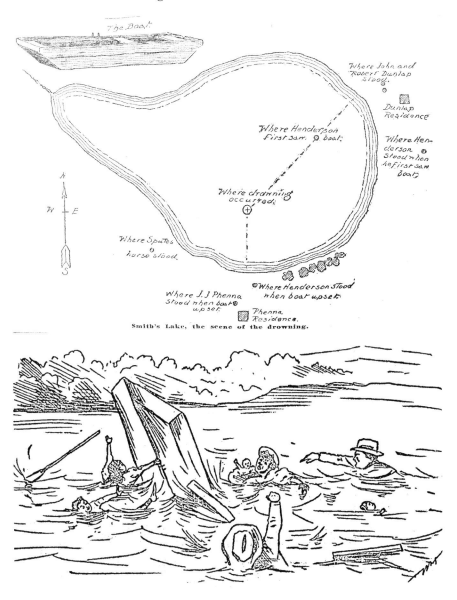

Smith's Lake, with location of the boat indicated.

which stated that the insurance could only be collected in the event of her death, under duress from her husband. When speaking to the public regarding the matter of the insurance policy, Spute stated, "I wished to make the amount larger for the reason that she intended on a trip east and also intended camping in the mountains." The grossly overloaded boat, oddly enough, apparently aroused little suspicion.

On November 16, 1896, Spute was arrested and charged with killing his family for insurance money upon an indictment from the grand jury. Nellie Davis, age twenty-two, was arrested with him on the charge of being an accessory before the fact. Upon her arrest, she admitted that "Spute had maintained her in an elegant flat on Welton Street for over a year, and had on various occasions promised to purchase her a beautiful ten-thousand-dollar residence in the aristocratic part of the city." There was some uproar regarding his arrest, both by the public and by his personal friends, who claimed that the arrest was a conspiracy on the part of either the insurance agency or his lawyer and a detective agency.

According to newspaper reports at the time, the basis of the charge was the insurance money, as well as his secret double life; his relationship with Nellie Davis was said to be at least one-year old. Furthermore, it was stated that despite his statement that he could not swim, Spute was actually an excellent swimmer. Additionally, it was reported that his conduct at the funeral seemed unbefitting a recently bereaved husband. It was reported that when "the officiating clergyman invited the friends of the dead to step

Andrew Spute and his mistress, Nellie Davis.

forward and view the remains for the last time, he never moved out of tracks, and that he never shed a tear. He insisted upon keeping his store open on the day of the funeral."

Ultimately, Spute was released from jail after his pastor from the Swedish Lutheran Church, Reverend Gustaf Brandelle, secured a $5,000 bond for him. Possibly the staunch support of the church was influential. In any event, Spute's supporters began to rally and charged that he was the victim of a conspiracy on the part of the insurance company. Spute's arrest, they claimed, was a mere subterfuge to allow the company to avoid payment on the policy. Four witnesses came forward and claimed that the drowning was purely accidental and that Spute was convincingly distraught at the scene. The charges were eventually dropped, as sufficient evidence for an indictment was deemed to be lacking. Once Spute was no longer in fear of criminal charges, he filed suit against the Traveler's Insurance Company for his deceased wife's insurance money plus interest. He received $10,074.

Spute was not destined for domestic bliss. He did not marry Nellie Davis, and he left Denver. In 1906, he married Anna W. Spute, age twenty-one; he was then forty-five years old. They lived in Alaska, where he had some mining property, and then in Seattle, and finally they relocated to rural Kitsap County, Washington. There, Anna filed for divorce, alleging that Spute was abusive and unpleasant. The Washington court denied her the divorce, finding no grounds: "The whole trouble seems to be that the plaintiff wishes to live in Seattle rather than live on a farm." Anna appealed the case to the Washington Supreme Court, which reversed the lower court judgment in 1913 and ordered it to enter a decree of divorce. Moreover, Spute was ordered to pay Anna $1,250. He died in Bremerton, Washington, on October 19, 1949.

KEMP BIGELOW

"Each bomb contained enough explosive to kill everyone within a radius of fifteen feet."

The early years of the twentieth century saw many bombing incidents. In Denver, bombings by paid labor terrorist Harry Orchard in Colorado in 1903 brought attention to "infernal machines" and, perhaps, an inspiration to others. One attempt at blackmail by explosive was the brainchild of Kemp V. Bigelow (aka Biglow), age twenty-one, a clerk at the Kendrick Book & Stationery store in Denver.

The recipients of the bomb packages (left) and Kemp Bigelow (right).

On October 7, 1907, Bigelow made an assassination attempt on several Denver notables—Governor Henry Buchtel; Charles B. Kountze, president of Colorado National Bank; David H. Moffat, president of First National Bank; Lawrence C. Phipps, millionaire (and later U.S. senator); and Ed Chase, "king of Denver's gambling syndicate"—by mailing bombs to the first four men and placing sticks of dynamite in the vacant lot next to Edward Chase's home.

Bigelow, a native of Byron, Ohio, became a suspect in these incidents when he appeared at the police station, claiming to have information regarding the case. In his first statement to the police on October 7, he stated that he had overheard some men planning to put bombs in the mail. However, under further interrogation, Bigelow confessed on October 9 to committing the crimes himself. According to one report, "The strongest piece of evidence against Bigelow besides his confession is the fact that through a clever trick of the local and Pinkerton detectives he was shadowed and seen to mail the bombs to the men whom he had warned the police would be assassinated."

During the interrogation, Bigelow claimed that he had no intention of hurting anyone but was simply seeking financial gain; he hoped that if he warned the recipients of the bombs, he would be rewarded. He also admitted to mailing letters to a number of companies, threatening to wreck trains

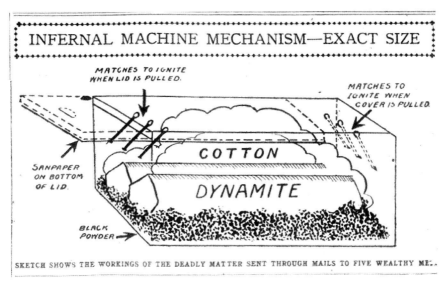

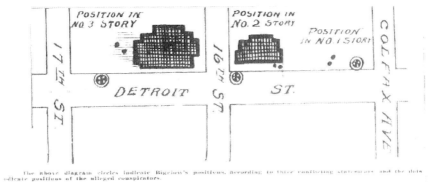

Bigelow's infernal machines.

unless his demands were met, although nothing had come of these threats. However, as the *Fairplay Flume* reported, "The bombs were so constructed that, had they not been intercepted, they might have exploded." The *Summit County Journal* asserted that "each bomb contained enough explosive to kill everyone within a radius of fifteen feet." Each bomb was designed to ignite when the package was opened; sliding the lid would strike the matches and set off the gunpowder within, and then the dynamite would explode.

During the criminal proceedings, Bigelow was first charged with assault against Moffat, to which he pleaded guilty. Bigelow's parents spoke publicly about their son; his father, who accompanied Bigelow to and from the courtroom, explained that his son had committed his crimes because he was "becoming insane."

On November 19, Bigelow was found guilty of simple assault on Moffat, an offense that carried a sentence of only sixty days in the county jail; however, the verdict was set aside on the grounds that it was contrary to the evidence. On December 14, 1907, Bigelow pleaded guilty on the charges of assault with intent to kill Governor Buchtel, Lawrence Phipps and Charles B. Kountze, as well as one count of operating a confidence game. Sent to the reformatory, he was paroled on September 17, 1908, and showed every indication of becoming "a fine young fellow," according to the warden. He left Colorado to take up a position as a bookkeeper in Chicago. His path ended as an inmate of a Veterans Administration facility for disabled soldiers in Bath, New York, where he died in 1940.

MRS. ALLEN READ

"I don't know who I am; I don't know where I am from. I came to Denver from somewhere in the east with Madame LeRoy."

Two unusual women were involved in a case that was front-page news in November 1908. The first, a demure druggist's wife, was consistently referred to by her married name, Mrs. Allen Read ("Reed" is used occasionally). Even her prison registers do not reveal her given name, but census records confirm that she was Frances "Fannie" Read (née Campbell), born in Pittsfield, Massachusetts. Read, age thirty-seven, appeared to be the essence of middle-class gentility, which made her actions all the more shocking. In November 1908, she attempted to extort $20,000 from Mrs. Genevieve Chandler Phipps, age twenty-nine, ex-wife of millionaire Lawrence C. Phipps (himself a victim of Kemp Bigelow's extortion scheme) by blackmail and death threats. As in the Bigelow case, explosives were involved.

Lawrence and Genevieve Phipps had been in the news repeatedly in Denver newspapers in 1904 as a result of their acrimonious divorce and custody battle. At one point, the two daughters of the marriage were kidnapped on Phipps's orders and taken to New York City; large sums of money were bartered back and forth as settlement offers. The extensive media coverage may have made them targets for extortion.

On November 9, 1908, Genevieve set out in her electric limousine to pick up her daughter Helen, age five, from school. She was hailed by a veiled

Genevieve Phipps.

woman as the chauffeur drove through City Park. The woman requested an interview with Genevieve, explaining that she was writing a book in collaboration with journalist/publisher Joseph Medill Patterson on socialism and society. Genevieve agreed to speak to her and offered her a ride in the car. Once the woman (who was Mrs. Read) entered the vehicle, she pulled out sticks of dynamite and informed Genevieve, "I'm desperate and must have money at once. I want $100,000." She directed the driver to go to the International Trust Company, a bank used by the Phipps family. First, they picked up Helen from school; Mrs. Read intended to use her as a hostage if necessary. On the drive, she rapidly reduced her demand to $20,000; once at the Equitable building, where the bank was located, she sent Genevieve in to retrieve the money and remained with Helen—and the dynamite—in the car.

Genevieve immediately informed a bank officer of the situation. A bank detective, John McDonald, went out to the car and greeted Helen. Mrs. Read warned him to go away, but he pulled Helen from the car. As he did so, Read hurled a stick of dynamite at him. It struck his head and snapped in two harmlessly. The police wagon arrived, and Read was taken into custody. Mrs. Read was charged with assault and battery. She was extremely distraught and attempted to swallow a handful of morphine tablets; she also claimed to be under the spell of a clairvoyant and unable to control her actions. "I don't know who I am; I don't know where I am from. I came to Denver from somewhere in the east with Madame Leroy," she stated. Madame LeRoy "had a strange influence over me and said she was going to help me…She was going to cure me of that terrible morphine habit." Both police and newspapers seized on this theory, speculating that Read had "come under the influence of some designing person who, by [hypnotic] suggestion, had induced her" to commit the crime.

As it transpired, Mrs. Read's path had apparently converged with that of Madeline LeRoy (or Leroy) Thompson (aka Madeline Langley) in the days before the crime. Thompson was a woman with a complex and surprising criminal past. She first came to the attention of the Denver authorities on January 20, 1900, when she was arrested for the theft of $80 from a man named W.G. Wolff. Thompson's statements to detectives were peculiar and almost rose to the level of confabulation. Bizarrely, she stated that she was only nineteen years old and was roundly disbelieved (she was actually thirty-five years old, according to her first husband). Describing herself as a gently reared convent girl from Atlanta whose guardian, a Chicago uncle, had died, she claimed that her weak lungs prompted her relocation to Denver. She married a man named A.G. Thompson there. While she was in possession of $500 for her "wedding trip" to Manitoba, she claimed that Wolff decoyed her into his room at 1862 Curtis Street, locked her in and robbed her of the money. (She was able to grab $75, but "Wolff got the rest.") She also alluded to a larger conspiracy to defraud her of her inheritance.

The attempt to turn the tables on the actual victim (Wolff) did not succeed. Instead, her true identity was revealed in the press. She was actually Mamie Starr (aka Ray or Emma Stark), a Chicago servant who had murdered her employers, Mr. and Mrs. F.W. Newland, by poisoning them with a product called Rough on Rats. On April 4, 1890, Starr mixed the arsenic-based poison into some canned corn and served it to the Newland family. The adults died two days later. The children—Grace, age sixteen, and Francis, age twenty-one—grew dangerously ill but recovered. Starr claimed that she had been depressed and bought the poison to take herself. She could not explain how it wound up in the corn, but she panicked when she realized that the Newlands were sick. She threw away the box, but her purchase was remembered at the drugstore, and she was arrested. She was tried for the crime, found guilty and sentenced to life in prison on January 3, 1891. Starr was released from the penitentiary on April 3, 1898, her term being commuted for good conduct.

Mamie Starr (left) and Madeline LeRoy Thompson (right). Are they the same woman? *Colorado State Archives.*

When viewing pictures of Thompson and Starr side by side, they do share a number of features, particularly a noticeably strong chin. Thompson, of course, utterly denied that she was Mamie Starr, despite an identification by Starr's husband, S.W. Ray—from whom, incidentally, she had never been divorced. Moreover, Mamie Starr was at least as extravagant a storyteller as Madeline Thompson. In spite of Thompson/Starr's creativity, she was found guilty of larceny and sentenced to a year in prison. Upon her release from prison for the Wolff incident, she reinvented herself as Madame LeRoy, a clairvoyant, and became Mrs. Read's mentor.

After Mrs. Read was examined by physicians, police released a statement to the effect that she appeared to be under hypnotic influence at the time of the offense. Read's husband confirmed her morphine habit and told the press that it was a byproduct of her tuberculosis and liver cancer. In fact, he suggested that Mrs. Read believed *herself* to be Madame LeRoy, which might have been the first split-personality defense had anyone paid attention to it. Her sister, who came to Denver from Massachusetts to lend her support, said that Mrs. Read's mind was unbalanced but that she was more suggestible than criminal. But where was Madeline Thompson/LeRoy? Police tried to find her, but she had disappeared—no doubt to re-create herself elsewhere.

Mrs. Allen Read. No first name was given, even on her mug shot. *Colorado State Archives.*

On November 19, Mrs. Read was charged with assault with intent to commit robbery and bodily injury to Genevieve Phipps. Her weakened physical health led to many delays in the judicial process, and her mental state was a primary issue in the trial. In November 1909, her case finally came before a jury. The trial was a battle of opinions as to Mrs. Read's sanity and drug addiction. Found guilty, her prison term was set at one to one and a half years. Upon her release on November 10, 1910, she was quickly removed to Pueblo, where she was reunited with her husband and reportedly left Colorado.

GENKYO MITSUNAGA

"There was every indication of a Japanese's work."

The Mitsunaga case centers on the 1910 murder of Katherine Wilson, age thirty-eight, by Genkyo Mitsunaga, age twenty-six. Katherine's body was discovered by her husband, real estate dealer Ridgely Wilson, and her daughter, Mabel Galland, on May 8, 1910, in her bungalow at 1054 Clayton Street. Ridgely had been in Hot Springs, Arkansas, while Katherine had remained in Denver to move into the newly rented house. She had arranged to meet a friend, Hazel Miller, on the evening of the seventh, but when Miller arrived, she found the house locked and no one at home. When Mabel and Ridgely searched the house the next afternoon, they found nothing. They left to go to Mabel's house when, as Ridgely testified later, "we went a little way down the street and then turned and came back. I don't know why we came back; but it seemed an irresistible impulse. When we got in the house I went into the cellar [searched earlier by Mabel]. At last, as I was about to leave the cellar, I chanced to notice the top of a shoe sticking out of a packing box—a large box—under the stairs." Katherine's strangled and beaten body had been stuffed into the packing. Police later found an "Indian club" spattered with blood and hair in the cellar; the hair color matched Katherine's.

Initially, the investigation focused on Katherine's ex-husband, John T. Higginson, whom she had divorced nine years earlier, as well as current husband Ridgely Wilson, but it was deemed that there was no real evidence that they were involved. However, at the time, Katherine's neighbors pointed out that Katherine had a Japanese man helping her prepare the house for occupancy. Moreover, "Mrs. Wilson was a big strong woman, and the apparent ease with which she was strangled and the strange marking of the forehead lead the police to believe that Oriental methods figured in the murder."

The Japanese man was Genkyo Mitsunaga, a housecleaner for the Broadway Cleaning Company, a Japanese employment agency located at 1148 Broadway. He became a suspect after it was discovered that he had been sent to clean her house that day and was the last confirmed visitor

Genkyo Mitsunaga. *Colorado State Archives.*

to the home. Suspiciously, he had disappeared from his workplace and lodgings. The company record book contained a partially obliterated entry; under magnification, it showed that Mitsunaga was assigned to the job at the Wilson house. Some reporters expressed doubt throughout the case that he strangled a "big strong woman" easily. Mitsunaga was five feet, one and a half inches tall and weighed 116 pounds; Katherine's height is unknown, but she weighed 170 pounds.

Mitsunaga was apprehended in McCook, Nebraska, on May 12, 1910; he was returned to Denver, delivered into police custody and arraigned in court on September 13, 1910. The charges were murder, accessory to murder and concealing the crime. At trial, the prosecution painted the case as a simple money dispute; Mitsunaga was unhappy with the amount Katherine paid him, and he strangled her. Defense attorney O.N. Hilton presented a different scenario and directed the jurors back to Ridgely Wilson. The trial was not without its irregularities. Testimony was disrupted several times by noisy spectators, who were removed from the courtroom. Evidence disappeared. The work clothes Mitsunaga wore on the day of the crime were handed over to police by his employer, but they turned up missing. Chief of Police Hamilton Armstrong testified that "they had been given to a janitor who had since died."

According to Mitsunaga, who testified via an interpreter, he was at work cleaning windows when the doorbell rang. He heard voices coming from the kitchen; the only words he distinguished were "Baby, baby," spoken by Katherine. Then he heard a thud. (The prosecutor found the relative lack of noise improbable.) A few minutes later, a white man came in the room and pointed a gun at him. The man ordered Mitsunaga to help him move Katherine's body, first taking out his handkerchief and tying it tightly around Katherine's neck. The two men carried the body downstairs to the cellar, where they dumped Katherine into the packing case. The white man covered up the body with straw and then led Mitsunaga back into the kitchen and told him to clean the blood off the floor. Mitsunaga complied; the man threatened him with death if he ever talked, gave him a roll of money ("I did not want it but he forced it on me") and left the house. Mitsunaga, frightened of both the man and the police, went back to the cleaning company office, changed his clothes and, acting on the advice of friends, left town.

Attorney Hilton made every effort to attach suspicion to Ridgely, first because of his "irresistible impulse" to re-search the cellar; further, Ridgely, after finding the body, had made a prescient pronouncement that a Japanese man was responsible for Katherine's death. When asked about the remark at

Katherine and Ridgely Wilson.

trial, he elaborated: "There was every indication of a Japanese's work. It was as plain to me as if it had been written in letters of fire on the wall. I smelled it; I felt it; I saw it. The stuffing of the body into the box, the abruptness with which the housecleaning had been left off, the cleaning up of the marks of the murder—all these things said 'Japanese housecleaner' to me. I still say that, and I will keep on saying it." (As preposterous as this statement sounds, the prosecutor adopted Ridgely's theory in his closing argument, declaring, "No English-speaking person would have committed that crime in that way.")

Other facts supported Ridgely's possible involvement. Evidence suggested that some clothing had been burned in the furnace of the Clayton Street house; Ridgely denied ever building a fire in the house. Reportedly Katherine had changed her will the day before her death, excluding Ridgely and leaving her entire estate to daughter Mabel. This, Hilton argued, was a motive for the murder. However, Ridgely had some documentation to support his Hot Springs trip, including a cancelled check and a baggage stub. (Years later, the *Colorado Springs Gazette-Telegraph* would report that Wilson's next wife, Virginia Durand, had filed for divorce, claiming that Wilson attacked her and her daughter with a butcher knife.)

Was Mitsunaga the killer? A neighbor testified to seeing a white man enter the Wilson house on the afternoon of May 7, but her testimony rambled and became so incoherent that the district attorney began an inquiry into her mental condition (in particular, her "denials to questions at times took the form of shrieks"). Mabel Galland believed that Mitsunaga was, at worst, an accessory after the fact. The Japanese community in Denver raised money for a psychological evaluation to assist his defense.

Ultimately, however, Mitsunaga was convicted of murder on December 9, 1910, and was sentenced to life at the Canon City penitentiary for Katherine Wilson's murder. A Japanese attorney, who had come to Colorado to try to clear Mitsunaga's name, took his case to the Colorado Supreme Court, but the verdict was upheld on January 6, 1911.

JOSEPH BRINDISI

"I won't say at this time that I did not do it, or I won't say that I did do it."

On August 27, 1923, the bodies of Lillian McGlone (aka Lillian Hudson), twenty-eight-year-old wife of athletic instructor Roy McGlone, and Emma Vascovie, age nineteen, were found dead from gunshot wounds to the head in room 2 of the Del Ray Hotel apartment building at 825 Delaware Street. A .38-caliber Colt revolver was lying on the floor between the bodies.

The scene initially puzzled investigators. Was it a murder-suicide, or were the two women killed by a third party? A scrawled, incoherent note was found on a dressing table in the apartment:

> *I kill him because I though to much of him I want him to going me where*
> *I go*
> *Good-by I am happy now*
> *–L*
> *She not to* [sentence unfinished]

Despite the signature "L," the handwriting was not Lillian McGlone's, and nor was the stilted English, which appeared to be written by a nonnative speaker. The note, officers concluded, was probably planted by the killer to misdirect the investigation. A glass half-full of brown liquid was also found

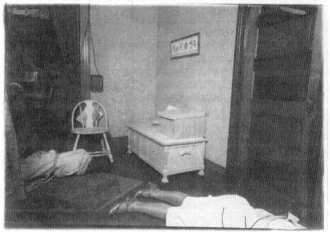

Inside the room at
the Del Ray Hotel.

on the dressing table; it was sent to be analyzed, as was a bloodstained cloth on a chair. Police also observed that there were powder marks on the victims' faces, indicating that they were shot at close range.

Lillian's husband of eight years, Roy McGlone, age thirty six, had been away in the mountains near Bailey on a camping vacation. When he heard of the deaths, he returned to Denver and informed police that Lillian lived in constant fear of a man known as "Joe," who had threatened to kill her several times. The gun used in the shooting, he added, belonged to the McGlones and was normally kept in their linen closet. Another statement was given by Lillian McGlone's brother-in-law, Alfred Calone, who told the police "of an Italian, the only person in the world…who could have

Left to right: Emma Vascovie, Lillian McGlone and Joseph Brindisi.

committed the crime." However, while newspapers reported that police were combing the Italian neighborhoods of Denver looking for a man named "Joe," the man had already been identified. The landlord at the Del Ray, Edmund "Gus" Hoglund, immediately directed police to Joseph Brindisi (aka Briendisse, Brandissi or Berny), age thirty, another tenant who had been closely associated with the women. Brindisi, formerly employed by the Morey Mercantile Company, had been laid off from his job; often described in the media as a "Sicilian," he was actually born in Colorado and was not of Sicilian ancestry.

Newspapers assumed that the McGlones made their home at the Del Ray, but it does not appear that this was the case. However, Lillian McGlone was a regular visitor to Brindisi's room (no. 15) and Vascovie's room (no. 18). Vascovie, a former laundry worker, had moved into the Del Ray in October 1922. The lack of current employment for all three parties had an explanation that did not make it into the newspapers: they were involved in the illicit sale of alcohol.

On March 24, 1924, Brindisi was located in Detroit, arrested and returned to Denver. During the trial, he stated that he had quarreled with McGlone on the day of August 25, given her a black eye and then later returned to her apartment on the morning of August 27. Although he declined to say what he did while in the apartment and refused to either admit or deny the crime (he replied, "I won't say at this time that I did not do it, or I won't say that I did do it," in response to questioning), he did state that he was at the residence for an hour and a half before leaving and throwing his gun in the creek at the Eleventh Avenue Bridge. He remained in Denver for a few days before going to Mexico. He returned to Denver in October and then went to Detroit on December 6, where he had used the alias "Frenchie LaBelle" and had been employed at a Dodge Brothers plant.

According to the trial testimony of the landlord of the Del Ray apartments, on August 25, 1923, McGlone, Brindisi and Vascovie had gathered in Vascovie's room; they spent several hours there drinking and quarrelling. McGlone was heard to say, "Go to hell, you damn son of a bitch." The landlord, Edmund Hoglund, appeared to feel that McGlone was the main source of the trouble and wanted her to leave the premises. McGlone protested, "That bastard there, he got a gun." Brindisi denied the allegation, and Hoglund told them, "You keep quiet here, otherwise you get out." Later, the three went out and were seen arguing in an alley near the hotel. In the early morning of the twenty-sixth, Brindisi went to a friend who was also staying at the hotel and told him that he had given McGlone a black eye. When the friend went to investigate, McGlone asked the man to take her home, but Brindisi would not allow it: "No, she is not going home until she settles with me."

Several hours later, Vascovie acquired a new room (no. 2) for herself and McGlone, allegedly to "get away from Joe." In the morning, the women went to Calone's house and remained there until Sunday night. During this time, Brindisi repeatedly called the residence, demanding to speak with McGlone; he was refused. On Monday, August 27, Calone took McGlone and Vascovie back to the Del Ray. While the women were sitting on the porch (McGlone with her black eye bandaged), Brindisi arrived, and he and McGlone went inside. As a side note, one witness, the landlady of the Del Ray Hotel, noted that Brindisi had put a pistol in his pocket before leaving the establishment earlier.

Shortly after McGlone and Brindisi went inside, Vascovie followed. Five minutes later, according to witnesses, there were several shots. At 5:30 p.m., a neighbor passed by the house and saw that the door to room no. 2 was ajar. Looking inside, he saw a woman's body on the floor. He notified the police, who arrived promptly to find Vascovie and McGlone dead on the floor.

In addition to the witness corroborating the story of Brindisi's abuse and threats against McGlone, the prosecution at the trial also introduced the handwritten note from the crime scene as evidence, comparing it with samples of McGlone's and Vascovie's handwriting; it matched neither.

In spite of efforts to focus the case on a McGlone-Brindisi love affair and murder caused by jealousy, there are many indications that a business

The Del Ray Hotel at 825 Delaware Street: front view (top), with murder room marked; and rear view (bottom).

relationship was at the heart of the case. The McGlone house, rather than the Del Ray, appears to have been the place where the bootleg alcohol was stored, and many of the activities of the principals involved trips to retrieve it. Both McGlone and Vascovie sold "moonshine whiskey" from the Del Ray, and Brindisi's comment that Lillian needed to "settle" with him almost certainly referred to a money payment—a debt or split of profits.

On the other hand, the defense also attempted to argue that, contrary to reports that Brindisi had threatened, abused and murdered McGlone, Brindisi had, in fact, been attacked *by* McGlone. The defense also stated that McGlone had been jealous of Brindisi's wife (later they divorced), had trailed her, beat her up and attempted to make Brindisi choose between the two of them. In the alternative, McGlone shot Vascovie and then committed suicide. All character evidence about McGlone was excluded by the judge, who reasoned that "there is no scrap of evidence admitted, or offered, tending to substantiate such a theory."

Despite the efforts of the defense, Brindisi was convicted of first-degree murder of McGlone and Vascovie and sentenced to life in prison. Later, his attorney applied for a writ of error to review the judgment of the district court; the original judgment was upheld on November 10, 1924. Brindisi died in Denver in 1981.

Chapter 9

The Perils of Everyday Life

N on-homicide offenses are more difficult to track. If records are sparse for murder cases, they are much more so for property crimes and misdemeanors. Nonetheless, some stories have survived, albeit in partial form, and they shed additional light on the everyday hazards of life in the time period.

LARCENY AND FORGERY

In the 1880s and 1890s, Denver experienced a boom in larceny cases. The *News* commented on one occasion when "the criminal court docket [was] crowded with cases of big and small stealing." Fred St. Clair, age eighteen, was a frequent visitor to criminal court. His official occupation was "varnisher," but he was also a proficient thief. Described by the *News* as "the leader of a gang of sneak thieves," he began his career in Warren, Pennsylvania. At age fourteen, he was sent to the reform farm for robbery and then released on condition that he leave the state. Fred and his parents, Charles G. and Avice St. Clair, moved to Denver.

Fred resumed his chosen career in the West. He entered residences in the afternoon and specialized in jewelry thefts. In March 1884, he faced twenty-one charges of larceny, having stolen nearly $10,000 worth of jewelry. He and his mother were tried in November 1884 for larceny and receiving stolen goods.

Avice, age thirty-eight, testified on Fred's behalf. She was "a woman of good features and genteel appearance" and "evidently shrewd and bright." This is

Avice and Fred St. Clair. *Colorado State Archives.*

not to say that her testimony was necessarily believed: "She said that she was a vocalist and a teacher of vocal music, and that her husband was a violinist and prominent mover in musical circles, meaning, probably, a piano mover." Avice told the story of how Fred, at age five, received a blow on the head from a falling piece of coal. Before the wound healed, he received another head injury. After that time, he began to steal small things when at school. The stealing never stopped, and Fred was a kleptomaniac thereafter. Regardless, on December 23, both Avice and Fred were convicted. Avice was sentenced to five years in prison and Fred to six. We have no release date for Avice, but Fred was discharged on December 31, 1887.

A forger named Joseph Gilligan (aka James or Maude Gilligan, Arthur or Clara DeRemer or Deemer), age nineteen, a tailor by occupation, was also given a large share of news coverage, perhaps because his methods were unusual and generally effective. Gilligan was a skilled and convincing female impersonator. He was arrested several times in the 1890s for similar offenses, some committed as his female alter egos, "Maude Gilligan" or "Clara DeRemer."

Joseph Gilligan (left) and Elmer Brown (right). *Colorado State Archives.*

In Colorado Springs in December 1891, Gilligan forged checks in the names of A. Hemenway and J.I. Sellers for $25.00 and $14.00, cashed them and went to Denver. Once there, he passed another forged check at Nichols Brothers musical instrument dealers at 1551 Champa Street for $14.50, as well as another at Pell's Restaurant for $7.00. In January 1892, he was sentenced to four years in prison for both the Colorado Springs and Denver incidents.

Discharged on March 16, 1895, Gilligan was soon back at his trade. On April 24, Gilligan and accomplice Elmer E. Brown (aka Frank Miller), age twenty, were arrested at their room at 1312 Tremont Street and charged with embezzlement and forgery in the amount of $3,000. This time, the forged checks were passed at the Western Hotel and the Moore Shoe Company. In addition, the pair had rented two pianos, from the Knight-Campbell Music Company and the Denver Music Company, respectively. The two men then attempted to obtain chattel mortgages on the pianos, but the money brokers became suspicious and notified the music firms.

Police and reporters had a field day with the discovery of women's clothing and provocative letters. The *Post*'s headline on April 25 was "A Queer Case, This," and the article's first sentence read, "Denver has a real Oscar Wilde, and he languishes behind the prison bars of the city jail." Allegedly, detectives thought they had been sent to a ladies' room on Tremont Street: "A richly made street dress, corsets and two complete changes of lady's underwear, a yachting cap and heavy blue veil adorned the closet. On the dresser, powder, hair curler and penciling for the eyebrows, lady's [*sic*] No. 5 shoes, gloves, dainty handkerchiefs and incenses that go to complete a lady's boudoir were found." The letters were quoted extensively, probably because they contained endearments to and from Gilligan and other men. A notebook with names and addresses of well-known Denver citizens was also mentioned, along with the suggestion that Gilligan had been engaging in or contemplating blackmail. Brown, a plumber by trade, had been released from prison at the same time as Gilligan, after serving four years for robbing a jewelry store in Pueblo; he and Gilligan would pose as a husband and wife on their shopping excursions.

Gilligan was arrested again on April 30, 1896, for forging checks in the name of his employer, Mrs. L.E. Gillman, and passing them at two grocery establishments. He appeared next in California, where he moved in succession from county jail (writing bad checks, larceny) in 1900 to the San Quentin penitentiary in 1910. Gilligan ran afoul of a mandatory minimum sentence for a person with three convictions for forgery: fourteen years in prison. In Denver, he was succeeded by a young man named Earl Williams (aka Pearl Williams or Beatrice Farley), who gained some notoriety in June 1912 for an equally successful female impersonation: "He committed many crimes while disguised as an innocent girl."

Shoplifters: The Watson Gang

In 1897, the *Denver Post* stated that "'Shoplifters' are becoming so numerous in this city that the managers of the large stores will meet next week to formulate a plan for protection from these thieves." Proposed solutions included more store detectives and deputized clerks who could arrest shoplifters on the spot. However, a detective (unnamed) blamed the store managers themselves for failing to pursue prosecution and for keeping their goods in such confusion that theft was easy. He made mention of the "notorious Watson gang" as the last case of "serious trouble" involving shoplifting.

The Watson Gang consisted of Jacob Watson, age thirty; his wife, Annie Watson (aka Grace), age twenty-seven; Tillie Williams (aka Lillie, Nellie, Minnie or Tillie Naylor), age twenty-six and possibly Annie's sister; and Otto Reinche (aka Herman Reinch), age twenty-one, sometimes

The Watson Gang. *Left to right*: Tillie Williams, Otto Reinche, Annie Watson and Jacob Watson. *Colorado State Archives.*

identified as Annie and Tillie's brother. As the parties were eager to put out misinformation about themselves, much of their biographical information is contradictory. Officially, Tillie was a housekeeper, Annie a dressmaker, Otto a confectioner and Jacob a cable car conductor.

"The most celebrated case of shoplifting" in Denver began on December 23, 1892, when Tillie and Annie were arrested for stealing silk dress goods from the Flanders dry goods store (they seem to have tucked them into their clothing); they gave false names at the station and feigned outrage and faintness. Jacob, in the meantime, reported his wife as missing, since she had not returned home. He did not find her until the next morning. At their hearing, both women pleaded for clemency, citing their small children, and the judge dismissed the case. However, they were arrested again a few days later for a similar offense. This time, they were each fined twenty-five dollars plus costs. Detectives were suspicious of their apparent familiarity with the courts and investigated further. After observing the women for a few days, warrants were obtained to search the Watson house at 242 Caithness Avenue, where all four adults and several children lived.

The raid took place in early January 1893. Police found the house not only well furnished but also "stacked with stolen goods from cellar to attic." When they first approached, Annie locked the door and began burning items in the stove. When police gained entry, they found pieces of express receipts for property shipped to Chicago, Illinois, and Spokane, Washington. Much of the stolen property was shipped to those cities and sold there; however, representatives from many Denver stores—Daniels & Fisher, the Golden Eagle, McNamara's, Salomon's, the May, Joslin's and so on—came to the house to locate and reclaim their goods. Many articles could not have been obtained by simple shoplifting and were probably obtained by burglary.

In February 1893, the two women and the Watson children all contracted scarlet fever while in the county jail and were ordered to the city hospital. This incident gave the *News* a chance to describe them more fully, since they objected vigorously to their removal. Annie (referred to as the "Queen of Shoplifters") assaulted the jail matron, Sadie Likens, and Tillie attempted to grab her keys: "It took four men to overpower and put the belligerent women in dungeons." The *News* continued, setting a dollar value on the offense: "They are two of the most notorious criminals ever captured in the west. They are accused of stealing $10,000 worth of dry goods. Shoplifting is their art and they have made a success of it."

The four gang members were put on trial, but when jury deliberations ended on March 18, only Otto was found guilty of receiving nine pairs of pants, two vests and one suit of clothes, all worth forty dollars and stolen from the May Shoe and Clothing Company on December 31. He was sentenced to three years in prison. Jacob, Annie and Tillie were discharged but were immediately rearrested on the charge of stealing lace curtains valued at thirty dollars from Daniels & Fisher.

All four were tried again in July, this time on conspiracy charges; they were found guilty and sentenced to prison terms in Canon City. The judge remarked that it was "a very peculiar case," in which the gang operated systematically as a business: "It is altogether different from the stealing of a loaf of bread for necessity, or the taking of a diamond pin worth $1,000 because of the impulse of the moment." As a warning to professional thieves and for the protection of the community, Tillie, Annie and Otto received ten years each. Jacob, whose guilt was mostly by association, received a six-year sentence.

In December 1893, news from the state penitentiary involving Tillie and Annie brought another scandal to light. Tillie and Deputy Warden Harry Bruce (son-in-law of Governor Davis H. Waite), who was in charge of the women's department, became involved in a flirtation or affair. As a result, she and Watson were given extraordinary privileges. Then, "in a fit of jealousy the Watson woman wrote to Warden Frank A. McLister, exposed Bruce and told of the disgraceful orgies which Matron Holzhouser permitted the negro women to indulge in. This caused much trouble and was the indirect cause of the penitentiary scandal which has disgraced the state." The matron was fired. Her superior, Bruce, was "severely lectured" and then discharged, and then he attempted a bizarre coup at the prison. "To save Bruce from further ignominy," Governor Waite dropped charges of malfeasance against McLister.

In June 1899, the *Post* reported that Tillie's husband, Henry Naylor of Chicago, discovered his wife's whereabouts. Their two older children—William, age fourteen, and Emma, age twelve—had been adopted by two Denver families. The younger children—Grace, age eight, and Harry, age ten—were still at the orphans' home, where young Grace was already showing the "hereditary" taint of her family. She had committed several small thefts, and "the fever in her blood may be too strong to check and the scheme of heredity may thrive in her frail body unto succeeding generations."

UNUSUAL CHARACTERS

Another colorful incident involved May Delyska (aka Delyski, Delesky or Deleski), age thirty, a Danish widow. Almost every detail of her past is subject to question. By one account, she was married to Anthony Delyska, who died in 1894. She lived for fifteen years in Ogden, Utah, and worked at the Troy laundry. Later, when she told her story to the Danish vice-consul, she had arrived in America from Aarhus only five years before. She seemed to thrive on ambiguity and misunderstanding.

In March 1896, Delyska was briefly employed as the housekeeper for two bachelors, William Erwin Davis and Isaac Ward Gardner, of 3131 Stout Street. Within a day, she had accused them of criminal (sexual) assault.

William, age thirty-two, was the son of a New York City millionaire, Erwin Davis; the latter had been in the news because of an inheritance dispute involving his brother's $10 million Montana estate. The Davis family was not just rich—they were very rich. Delyska might or might not have been aware of this. Davis was described as "mentally weak" and "an invalid from a particular nervous trouble for ten years." Ward, as he was known, had also come to Colorado in poor health. The Gardners and the Davises were friends, and the senior Davis had arranged for Ward to act as William's traveling companion/nurse. The men rented four rooms on the upper floor of the Stout Street house and had lived there for two months. According to Ward, an acquaintance told him that Delyska was looking for housekeeping work; he met with her at the Centennial Hotel, where she was staying, and hired her as their housekeeper for $5 per week.

Things went wrong very quickly. Delyska's first day at work was Friday, and by Saturday she had sworn out a warrant for the arrest of William and

May Delyska.
Colorado State Archives.

Ward. According to her story, she had been forced to spend Friday afternoon in William's room and then was subjected to "ill treatment" that night by Isaac. She was unable to escape until the next morning.

Ward denied any inappropriate conduct and, according to *the Rocky Mountain News*, averred that "Young Davis is almost an idiot, and he will say anything, and no reliance is to be put in his words." He had hired Delyska with no knowledge of her background. In his account, she came to the residence on Friday afternoon, cooked and served breakfast Saturday morning and then disappeared. "Then we were surprised by being arrested," he concluded. Their neighbor, a Mrs. Wilbraham, promptly posted bail for the men.

The case was dismissed. Delyska took up lodging with Mrs. Billington, a former police matron. One day, she disappeared, taking the matron's clothes with her. Arrested in May 1896 in Orrin Junction, Wyoming, she was returned to Denver, tried and found guilty of grand larceny. On June 17, she was sentenced to a term in the penitentiary. Discharged in May 1897, she resurfaced in Denver in October, working as a chambermaid at the Mascot home at Fifteenth and Market Streets. A lodger there, Christ Jackson, reported that $600 was missing from his room and that she was the only person who could have taken the money. She was arrested, but the charges were dropped.

The behavior of some defendants in court brought their cases more attention. Opium addict James Bolton, age thirty-five, occupation stenographer, appeared there on April 18, 1898, charged along with Joseph Trevithick for the holdup and robbery of William Holmes at Twenty-third and Champa Streets on March 4. They detained Holmes at gunpoint, relieved him of six dollars, his watch, a chain and a knife and left him tied to a tree. Holmes gave a good description of the men to police, and the two were arrested the next day.

Bolton had served six years in the Wyoming penitentiary and additional terms in New Mexico and Nebraska. In spite of his burly appearance in his mug shot, he was only about five feet tall and weighed 136 pounds. Bolton

James Bolton. *Colorado State Archives.*

154

was obviously well known in the Denver criminal court. On this occasion, he slumped from his chair to the courtroom floor and announced, "I've enough opium in me to kill me in twenty minutes. No use to go on with this trial. I'm a dead man." The judge replied, "That will do now. We've had your shamming before." Bolton continued, "I'm dead. Stop this stuff. It's all over with—" The judge snapped, "If you don't keep still I'll see that you are made to do so." Nonetheless, he sent for the county physician (who, incidentally, was not found). Bolton fell asleep within five minutes; he had apparently been able to obtain opium in jail. He had written a confession and stored it in his sock, but "it was not particularly valuable as the evidence against both prisoners was conclusive of guilt."

The *Post* noted that "Bolton has played the suicide game plenty of times in the last ten years." He and Trevithick were convicted of highway robbery; both were sentenced to fourteen years in prison. Once at the penitentiary, Bolton convinced the warden that he was insane. He was transferred to the Pueblo Asylum. On July 5, 1899, he escaped, as many inmates of the asylum were wont to do.

Of course, there were so many incidents of larceny in the city that some went virtually or completely unnoticed by the press. When a property crime involved a physical attack, it became newsworthy. On June 2, 1903, Lena Brown, age eighteen, was charged with highway robbery for slugging and robbing Joseph Daley of $400. Daley's skull was fractured. Brown's boyfriend, Green Watson, was also implicated in the assault. She also

Convicted of property crimes in July and September 1903. *Left to right*: Pearl Smith, age twenty-seven (larceny); Frank Chamberlain, age nineteen (burglary); and Lena Brown, age eighteen (robbery and larceny from person). Only Brown's case received any attention from reporters. *Colorado State Archives.*

attempted to pickpocket Herman Blazer and fought with detectives when she was arrested. The *Republican* noted, "The girl is considered a desperate character." Brown probably came from Topeka, Kansas, as her parents and listed contacts were living there. An interesting detail about her was that she had "scars on both hands from extra little fingers being amputated," according to her records. She was sentenced to one to two years in prison for robbery and larceny from the person in July 1903. Released in March 1905, she vanished from view, possibly—we hope—into a less desperate life.

About the Authors

S heila O'Hare, MA, JD, MLIS, is an assistant professor at Emporia State University and a former Denver resident. Alphild Dick, MA, is a graduate student at Emporia State University.

Visit us at
www.historypress.net